OUTSIDER IN THE VATICAN

Sistine Chapel during the Conclave

Outsider in the Vatican

By FREDERICK FRANCK

WITH 82 DRAWINGS BY THE AUTHOR

The Macmillan Company, New York

Collier-Macmillan Limited, London

The Macmillan Company, New York
Collier-Macmillan Canada, Ltd., Toronto, Ontario

Library of Congress catalog card number:
65-22617

Printed in the United States of America

First Printing

Acknowledgments

I OWE THANKS to all those Beatitudes, Eminences, Excellencies, Protestant Observers, Reverend Mothers, priests, monks, officials, gendarmes, journalists, who—knowingly or unknowingly—made it possible for me to be the most unofficial observer at the 21st Ecumenical Council, Vatican II.

"Conservatives" or "Progressives," their kindliness and courtesy have been immense. Without them, neither drawings nor text could ever have come about.

I owe thanks to those who kindly read my manuscript and whom I do not mention by name in order to save them, perhaps, embarrassment.

Humbly I ask forgiveness of those whose feelings I may inadvertently have hurt, for I fully realize my audacity as a non-theologian, a non-Catholic, a layman, and an artist, in reporting (be it peripherally on a drama in which all the actors are professionals and all the professionals, specialists.

Though I met innumerable people, delegated or paid to participate in the Council, to observe it, to describe it, I did not meet a single self-appointed brother-observer, one sufficiently foolhardy to rush in where angels feared to join the dance on the needle's point.

I remained a lone, self-made private eye, probably astigmatic, and armed only with a pen. I reacted as I could not help reacting, identified myself ever more with the events as I became involved more and more deeply.

I found myself perplexed at being perhaps the one representative of that vast unqualified world outside—unworthy, prejudiced, unscholarly—yet drawn irresistibly by hope, love, and an artist's curiosity to this century's mightiest religious event.

Contents

OUTSIDER IN THE VATICAN

Prologue

I T W A S not a whim. It was not an artist's search for sensational subject matter that made me "artist-in-residence" at the Council.

It was something quite different! I can hardly believe it now: on that twelfth of October, 1962, I was on my way to an appointment. As I walked along a New York City street I glanced at the headlines in *The New York Times.* I started to read Pope John's opening speech to the Council. Suddenly I felt an overpowering impulse to go and draw his Council—such an irresistible pull to Rome that I dropped all I was doing, the book I was writing, the paintings I was working on, and flew to Rome.

I had obeyed the overpowering impulse but did not understand it. Up to the very moment I read Pope John's opening speech I had scarcely been interested in this Council. Once arrived in Rome, however, I realized why I was there: I had come to settle an account.

The account to be settled was an old love affair that had started in early childhood and had—as too early loves often do—turned into an unhappy one.

Meeting the first-beloved by chance after many years, one finds oneself grimacing at a stout, carping housewife. When I met this old love again, she looked as young and fresh as ever. In fact, miraculously, she had grown more beautiful. The face I remembered as withdrawn and austere had become soft, motherly, radiant.

She had just resolved, she said, to start a new chapter in her life.

My love affair with the Roman Catholic Church had begun and—as I believed—ended on the borders where I was born and grew up—that strange point where the frontiers of Holland, Belgium, and Germany meet. Actually, it was a multiple border of nationalities, languages, cultures, and religions. Not just three countries meet there, but five languages. In my home town of Maastricht you learned Dutch in school, but with your friends you talked the Limburg dialect, an ancient dialect of the Duchy of Burgundy, offshoot of the medieval Low German of the Rhineland, generously sprinkled with Dutch, Flemish, and French. A mile to the south of my home town French was spoken exclusively. (Or rather, unofficially, the people spoke Walloon, an ancient Romance dialect belonging to the same group as Picard, Lorraine, and the Frankish, which was to develop into French.) A mile to the west, Flemish was the vernacular, and a few miles to the east, toward Aachen, the dialect became more and more German.

On such a linguistically unique home-ground you learn in earliest childhood to adjust your vocal chords, your lips, and your tongue according to the requirements of the language spoken, but that is not all: You learn at the same time to vary your very facial expression, your very gesturing, to harmonize with the German, French, or Dutch you speak.

To us border people it is natural, this early training in the relativities of expression, this proficiency in the mimicry of word, tone, and gesture so utterly strange to those who have grown up in neighborhoods or suburbs where people seem to be pressed from the same cultural mold, speak the same language, eat the same food, and go to the same church. To those linguistically more provincial, such cosmopolitan ease of communication looks quite suspect.

Having been born on borders, I was early aware of their irrelevance, as well as of their momentousness. I knew the border posts, where uniformed Belgian, German, and Dutch customs officers sat shivering in their little huts around coal stoves or lay in the fields chewing on sprigs of grass, lazily waiting for smugglers. At the same time, I knew that those borders were delusions. The same plants grew on both sides of the line, and in time of peace cows could be seen grazing on our side and throwing big fountains of dung on theirs, or vice versa, without partiality. The grass was the same, the peasants were the same, the gravel, the bread, the chocolate bars were the same—or nearly so. For the shape of Belgian loaves and the texture of Belgian chocolate frequently were subtly, deliciously different. And there was a pungent, infinitesimal difference in the smell of people, houses, signposts, and beer, a delicious and exciting shade of difference.

People from the center of a country see the border differently, of course. For them it is a political concept, or a principle, or a sinuous line on a map, It is the beginning of a foreignness to be criticized or imitated, the gateway to adventure. It is the place of egress or ingress, where uniformed men assert their authority and plunge tactless hands into neatly packed lingerie.

In times of war the border became a serious reality for us border people—a dangerous and poignant folly. It began for me for the first time when I was five years old. One day after Sunday dinner I walked at my father's side to look at the border, with big cannon roaring in the distance. The stone sugar loaf marking the border had the Dutch coat of arms on our side. A barbed-wire fence had just been built; behind it, with a bayonet, stood an old soldier of the German Landwehr. He looked like my father dressed up for the Mardi Gras ball, but he made me shiver with fear, and also pity. He was too old to stand so long in the drizzle in that too big greatcoat.

Soon, wounded soldiers streamed across the border—on foot, on horseback, or, all bandaged, on carts. Belgian, French, German, and even English and Russian soldiers were treated at our local hospital and then safely interned on our neutral soil. Too many found their way to us after their first taste of war, so the barbed wire was improved upon: It became electric wire, and the stream of soldiers stopped.

We hardly ever walked to the border then, but went only as far as the little chapel of St. Rochus, a tiny, hexagonal brick building about 6 by 6 feet on a crossroads under a big chestnut tree surrounded by wheat fields. It was closed off by a heavy iron door with rusty bars. Inside, amidst artificial pink roses and dense cobwebs, the saint was standing. He was a dusty, polychrome figure three feet high, who had lifted his brown plaster tunic to reveal a thin, muscular thigh torn by a hideous wound. At his feet lay a snarling dog. St. Rochus apparently did not suffer very much from his wound. His eyes were ecstatically rolled to Heaven in gratitude. Before the days of Louis Pasteur, St. Rochus had been the only protection against mad dog bites. In Holland, where rabies is extremely rare, St. Rochus had long been unemployed, victim of inexorable technical progress, in company with town criers, lamplighters, and coachmen. But I loved and revered him. He was the benevolent border guard of that other border I lived on, a border of religions. From early youth I had crossed it hundreds of times until the signposts were thoroughly familiar. Having been born in a veritable no-man's-land —an unstable mixture of decaying Protestant ethics and the weakest of Judaic atavisms—yet from earliest childhood surrounded by the wayside crosses, the chapels and churches of a Catholic earth, I was predestined for a religious border life.

I often think that we have asked all the great metaphysical questions by the time we are six, and never get much closer to the answers than we do then in our innocence. When I asked the questions, they were answered by the visible, audible, and indeed—there was always some odor of incense lingering—smellable presence of the Church in this beloved five-mile-square fatherland that straddled borders.

Maastricht thrived on processions and pilgrimages. There was always the last sacrament being rushed to the dying. At night, priests in lace rochets hurried by, carrying their holy burden, each preceded by an acolyte bearing a cross and a lantern. During the day their approach was announced by a silver bell, warning passers-by to kneel. Not being a Catholic I was not supposed to kneel, but my parents taught me to doff my cap "out of respect." To me it did not seem preposterous at all that here my undefined God was being brought to someone lying exhausted in his bed to make him ready for dying, saying, "See, I never left you; you just forgot about Me. Now that you are dying, know that I am by your side; I am inside of you. In Me you live on and I in you."

From as early as I can remember, the immense, sad crucifix on the wall of St. Servatius Cathedral, flanked by oil lamps in the dusk, bore down on me with its dark yet vaguely pertinent mystery.

I must have been five or six when I first saw the bejeweled miraculous statue of the Virgin from the ancient Romanesque church of Our Lady Star of the Sea carried in procession through the streets, in those years of war, epidemics, and stress, through throngs of silently praying people—my first intimation of religion as a "poetry of the soul."

On my way to school I used to pass the statue of the Sacred Heart at the entrance of the Cathedral, arms outspread in blessing. My little Catholic friends would take off their caps. "Only Catholics do that," my mother explained. I assumed that my friends greeted the statue itself, and did not realize that it was the consecrated Host behind him to whom they were paying their routine homage.

It was the embracing gesture of the statue that I loved. Each time I passed it, I secretly made the sign of the cross with two fingers over my heart, under my coat.

On my spiritual border, then, I was perhaps more Catholic than were my friends, but in absolute freedom. They inhabited the center of the Catholic country. For them the border was a thing far away, manned by guards in cassocks. Beyond it was the forbidden wasteland of heresy and unbelief. For them I was not *on* the border, but beyond it.

When I was twelve I had an inseparable friend with whom I went on daylong hikes through the Limburg hills. An anxious priest felt he had to speak sternly to the parents about this dangerous friendship with an unbeliever, and he broke it up.

The Church's border guard had closed the border and sealed it. I felt that he had denied my very humanity. His Church seemed to demand not just consent and love, but humiliating border formalities and a kind of naturalization that was equivalent to dishonorable surrender. I had already heard them talk about their "converts." I would stay on my side of the border!

From that moment on, my one-sided love affair with the Church became an unhappy one. How many love affairs with the Church through the ages have been ended by the aridity of its priests and the sycophancy of its laymen?

I was to live in Holland, Belgium, England, and America, and I took my border attitudes with me. Culturally I became ever more hybrid, more consciously eclectic, more convinced of the relativity of frontiers, more deeply affected by all attempts to build bridges across the abysses of delusion that separate us mortals, more loath to wear any label, national, cultural, or religious.

With multitudes of my contemporaries I shared a deep suspicion of all established religions, those institutions that prated constantly about God, Father to us all, while in His name instilling hostility, contempt, and hatred for those outside their particular fold. At the same time they cultivated a repulsive, collective self-satisfaction, a triumphalist egocentrism, within. In the little Holland of my youth, they demonstrated their insufferable imposture by the hardly veiled hatred between Catholics and Protestants, the naked animosity among fifty Protestant sects, each boasting of its exclusive monopoly on divine truth.

They seemed to be in league only when demanding a narrow, bourgeois, moralistic conformism, when hindering rather than stimulating that endless series of self-discoveries, of spontaneous movements toward depth-penetration that man is capable of and which he has to go through on his pilgrimage toward his Center. They offered their theological debris, their political maneuvers, their cultural atavisms as if these were the most exquisite gifts of the spirit, veritable elixirs of life. Instead of being the conscience of the world, the perpetually pointing finger to an existential experience of the Source of Life, they were content to exploit the finger as the focus of reverence, and they acted as hedges against man's specifically human need to experience his life. As if without it he could grow spiritually!

They seemed to insist on a theological anthropomorphism suitable for toddlers that offered adults little choice but total rejection. They carefully skirted the pressing moral issues of our time, of war and peace and hunger and race and leisure.

In my lone attempt at self-discovery I became an avid reader of Judaeo-Christian, Hindu, Buddhist, and Sufi literature until what matters about life clothed itself in formulations that might have come from St. Augustine, Eckhart, Ramakrishna, Hui Neng, or the Upanishads. Here I found the wonder at the miracle of our very existence transmitted, the intercourse of human consciousness with the source of all life clarified; I found compassion for man's fate, reverence for his search for existential light in his darkness. Regardless of forms and formulations, man's obstinate awareness of his spiritual potential, his abiding concern with the meaning of his existence, his compulsion to search in awe for the root of his being and for consciousness of his participation in all-life appeared, after all, as his most venerable, yes, redeeming, quality.

If there is any meaning in the saying that man is made in God's image, it must mean that he is born creative. This creativity may develop or it may wither. Man is also born with a calling to self-transcendence, to conscious communion with his source. This could not possibly mean the obligation to join one of these juridical, clerical bodies competing with each other. Nevertheless, his religions, however institutionalized and petrified, seemed to contain all his intuitions of that esthetic-moral-spiritual continuum of values without which he remains subhuman.

Being an artist, drawing and painting in Europe, Africa, and America, I exulted in the varieties of landscape, the widely diverse forms of plants and animals and of human faces. I rejoiced in the endless variations on life's basic structural themes. The exotic seemed to be no more than an optical illusion caused by unfamiliarity and distance. As I had learned in the microcosm of my border fatherland in childhood, the oneness of the land stretched unbroken under and beyond the electrified barbed wires.

At various periods of my life, nevertheless, a nostalgia for my first love invaded me. A Burgundian Madonna, a mass by Bach, Palestrina, Fauré or Messiaen, an enlightened Catholic magazine, such as *Esprit,* a poem by Péguy, a novel by Bernanos, a wayside cross in Brittany, the crypt of Vézelay, were enough to awaken this nostalgia. But it never lasted long, for soon there would be a concordat with Hitler in the making; German bishops would silently acquiesce in the mass murder of Jews; Spanish prelates were staunchly supporting the Falange; Italian cardinals had themselves photographed blessing the bombers that were off to "erase" Ethiopian villages.

And so, disenchanted and saddened, I began to see the beloved of my childhood as a fat, bigoted *entrepreneuse,* loaded with furs, waddling self-righteously through this appalling century, shaking a fat, bejeweled finger at little girls with too deep necklines while making eyes at politicians and hucksters, curtseying demurely to murderous dictators.

After the election of Pope John XXIII, human sounds seemed to be coming from Rome, but I was not going to be beguiled again.

Then, in the autumn of 1962, when once more the air was thick with threats of war, when it seemed that once again our world was on the brink of imminent final destruction, an old Pope spoke to the world from Rome. In a powerful affirmation of man's destiny—a prophecy of coming human unity in the face of all dire threats—he extended both hands across all borders in an irresistible gesture of conciliation. Through him, the Church, that lost love, suddenly appeared in her primal radiance. A prophet had arisen and had made all things new.

First Session

"In the daily exercise of Our Office, We sometimes have to listen, much to Our regret, to voices of persons who, though burning with zeal, are not endowed with too much sense of discretion or measure. . . . In these modern times they can see nothing but prevarication and ruin. They say that our era, in comparison with past eras, is getting worse. . . . They behave as though at the time of former Councils everything was a full triumph for the Christian idea and life and for proper religious liberty. . . . We feel We must disagree with these prophets of doom who are always forecasting disaster, as though the end of the world were at hand. . . ."

I READ this on October 12, 1962, a sunny day darkened by terrible forebodings. The prophets of doom had succeeded in persuading me that the end of our world could indeed be expected at any moment.

I was walking up Fifth Avenue reading *The New York Times.* I was on my way to an appointment with my editor at Macmillan to talk about a new book I was writing. It seemed pointless:

Commander Walter M. Schirra had just orbited this restless globe six times in his capsule, while Barnett C. Ross, governor of Mississippi, in violation of federal court orders, had blocked the admission of a Negro student at the state university. "I am moved by deep and abiding affection for the welfare of all the people of

Mississippi," the demagogue had declared proudly. Meanwhile the newspapers offered hopeful articles about our impending conquest of the moon.—Algeria's Ahmed Ben Bella, then premier, had announced his brotherly visit to Fidel Castro.—Former President Eisenhower was bragging that during *his* administration "no walls were built, no threatening foreign bases were erected."

In these last few weeks the bases were not only built, but photographs had appeared of missile sites in Cuba, provisionally labeled "defensive" by a nervous American government. At the same time the Berlin crisis was expected to boil over in the very near future. Had not *Pravda* declared that it was "imperative" that the question of a German peace treaty and the resulting adjustment of the situation in Berlin be settled "at once"?

In this atmosphere the Soviets announced new rocket tests in the Pacific; Peking was accusing India of border attacks; barbarous fighting had again erupted in the Congo; there was a revolution in Yemen in which Egypt, Jordan, and Saudi Arabia were busily stirring, threatening a major explosion in the Near East. To intensify this atmosphere of impending doom, the Soviets had warned in September that any attack on Cuba would mean war, and President Kennedy had countered that the launching of a nuclear missile against any nation in the Western Hemisphere would be met by retaliation by the United States against the Soviet Union.

Walking along a New York street I read that an eighty-one-year-old pope in Rome had calmly declared:

"Divine Providence is leading us to a new order of human relations, which, by man's own efforts and even beyond his very expectations, are directed toward the fulfilment of God's superior and inscrutable designs."

It was fantastic. It was so fantastic to read this quiet, impassioned message that I started to tremble with emotion. Pope John's words continued:

"We see in fact, as one age succeeds another, that the opinions of men follow one another and exclude each other. And often errors vanish as quickly as they arise, like fog before the sun. . . . Nowadays . . . the Spouse of Christ prefers to make use of the medicine of mercy rather than that of severity. . . . She considers that she meets the needs of the present day by demonstrating the solidity of her

teaching rather than by condemnations. . . ." He noted that *"men . . . are ever more deeply convinced of the paramount dignity of the human person"* and that *"violence inflicted on others, the might of arms, and political domination are of no help at all in finding a happy solution to the grave problems which afflict them."*

That morning an acquaintance had nervously called me to ask if I would consider renting him part of my small farmhouse north of New York "just in case of an emergency." "It is not to escape from the bomb in New York," he had explained, "but if anything happens I'd like my wife and child not to be caught in the panic."

"It is time," Pope John had said at that hour, *"that something decisive was done. For men* are *brothers, and, We say it from a full heart, all sons of the same father."*

Instead of offering new definitions of the exact place of the stray sheep in the Mystical Body, he had allowed Cardinal Bea to pray with Buddhists, Hindus, Protestants, and Jews in an agape, a love feast of human unity.

"Venerable Brothers," he exclaimed, *"such is the aim of the Second Vatican Council, which consolidates the path toward that unity of mankind which is a necessary foundation in order that the earthly city may be brought to resemble that heavenly city where truth reigns, charity is law. The Council now beginning rises in the Church like daybreak. It is now only dawn."*

In a review read that morning of a timely new book, *Kill and Overkill,* by Ralph F. Lapp, the author was quoted: "If country A loses 30 million dead and 27% of its economy, whereas country B has 90 million dead and 68% of its economy destroyed, the computer pronounces country A the winner. One wonders how much consolation that would be to country A."

"It is now only dawn."

The trembling inside of me had given way to a kind of exultation, as if the vulgar din of threat and counterthreat of mass murder had been drowned in an all-encompassing stillness. Yet all that had happened was that at last a human voice had succeeded in making itself heard, and had embraced a desperate world in old words of hope, reconciliation, and love—old words suddenly made new.

I found myself in a telephone booth and heard my voice saying to my editor: "Bob, I can't make it today. I am off to Rome. I want to draw at the Ecumenical Council. . . ."

My friends laughed at my bland assumption that I would be able to penetrate that "closed shop," gate-crash where priests without special qualifications had no chance to enter, where Catholic journalists loaded with credentials from omnipotent press agencies were powerless.

How could I, an artist, a non-Catholic—not even a "separated brother"—be so naïve as to waste my time and money, believing that I could simply walk into the Council with a sketchbook under my arm!

"So you are going on a Vatican safari," one of my friends said, smiling ironically. "Just remember that it is much more hazardous than your African ones. That *Città del Vaticano* is full of boa constrictors and puff adders!"

"Are you already a convert, or are you coming back converted?" There were dozens of variations on this theme, all of them betraying a profound uneasiness. I began to notice how acquaintances who had always expressed themselves quite forcefully in speaking of things Catholic became suddenly circumspect in choosing their words: they already considered me as belonging in the other camp. A few became so reserved that we lost all contact. An old friend silently slunk away as if he found something treacherous, obscene, in my preoccupation.

It was astonishing—and Catholics can't possibly realize to what extent—how deeply troubled, uneasy, and partial non-Catholics are where the Church is concerned. Hardly anyone was indifferent or was willing to have an open mind, I discovered.

All right, then, it would be a "safari into the Vatican." I would try to venture as deeply as possible into the interior. I was not quite unqualified, after all. For in Africa, during three long periods of work at Albert Schweitzer's hospital, and in Ethiopia, Sudan, Sierra Leone, Congo, Gambia, Ghana, and Nigeria, I had indeed ventured into the interior. I had learned there that all safaris lead into the same interior: one's own.

All safaris are safaris of the spirit or they remain vain pursuits of sensation; all safaris lead to the same reality, one's own existential reality, or, as one might put it, the encounter with one's God.

The plane landed at the Roman airport of Fiumicino at two o'clock in the morning on black concrete that was glistening in a cold, piercing drizzle. The airport bus, nearly empty, hobbled through the watery night, swallowed chunks of endless wet suburb in its dancing circle of light, bolted through desolate, black back-streets, to the terminal. A disgruntled taxi driver overcharged me and let me off at the Hotel Michelangelo, a characterless modern hotel near the Vatican. The vicious-looking night porter showed me to a much too elegant room in motel-modern style, with formica tops, a "sanitized" toilet, heated towel racks. Expensive and probably all-American.

A sudden anxiety took hold of me in that impersonal, un-European room. After all, whom did I know in Rome? I had to confess, to myself at least, that I knew nobody of any importance at all. An old friend in Holland, a baron who had once shown me a snapshot of himself in the Renaissance dress of a Chamberlain of the Sword and Cloak to the Holy Father, had promptly sent me a few of his cards with kind words of introduction. One to a Curia archbishop, the other to Brother Welsh, "a huge nice old Irishman who distributes tickets for papal audiences in the Office of the Maestro di Camera." Graham Greene had recommended a Roman count "who might have useful connections as one of his forebears was a Pope." My wife had remembered a relative, Jan Klooster, from her Catholic childhood in Holland, whom she had not seen for twenty years; he had become a bishop in Indonesia and should be at the Council. Bishop Klooster of Surabaja had answered that as a stranger in Rome he hardly knew his way around, but he asked me to come and see him at the mission house where he was staying. I would do that tomorrow morning. As I was falling asleep on my Roman bed, I suddenly looked on my adventure as a hopeless undertaking. I had followed my impulse. I had no further choice.

After a fitful sleep I woke up and opened my windows. Yes, I was in Europe; I was in Rome. A dense sheet of rain was falling over red-tiled roofs. From gray towers the ringing of bells entered my window. Bells sound different in the rain.

Downstairs in the lobby they were sitting—purple, gleaming, well-fed, florid bishops, reading breviaries and *Herald Tribunes,* freshly flown in from Paris—enjoying their free Saturday morning; no school until Monday! They drank coffee and exchanged desultory sentences in Midwestern accents: "Wet enough for you, Monsignor? It sure is coming down!"

Outside, the low, wet sky hung over autumnal Rome, chilling its two-thousand-year-old bones, drenching them. I had borrowed an umbrella from the day porter, who was all smiles and hopeful goodwill. The streets were greasy and wet, and the insanely scrambling scooters and Fiats behaved as if handled by half-drunken yokels on the Scooterama of a country fair.

I went on my first mission, and felt fainthearted and scared. I walked to the Casa della Missione on the Via Marcantonio Colonna, where Bishop Jan Klooster, of Surabaja, Indonesia, was staying. Through the façade the murky hollowness of the building was showing. It was now raining less demonstratively.

The door of the Casa della Missione was of wood, painted like imitation wood, and had cast-iron grillwork. In the drizzle the bell I pulled sounded cracked. A thin old man in an alpaca duster and slippers opened the door and disappeared to call Bishop Klooster, dragging his felt feet over the black-and-grey marble tiles. A mean electric bulb was glowing over the staircase. The waiting room was large and hollow, with a prie-dieu in a corner and a few yellowed photographs of cardinals, a pope, and the Vesuvius on the colorless wall. The chairs were like those I was to see later in all monastic reception rooms. Usually the wood was repainted a hideously synthetic walnut, going mad with artificial wood-nerves, the compulsive ornaments gilded with contemptible gold-bronze. Here they happened to be painted a dull, cheerless brown. It was terribly, audibly quiet. Yet outside the window, through the ornamented tulle curtains, I saw the slow rain descend on the unceasing race carried on by the flimsy cars.

The bishop came in, a tall man in his early fifties, dressed in a neat soutane with purple piping; his rather bony face had smiling, shy, grey eyes behind glasses. He was as quiet as the room. His handshake was very firm. He started: "I have been thinking what on earth I could do for you. You see, I don't know any important people around here. I am not exactly a Roman prelate! I am only a run-of-the-mill mission bishop and I just got here myself for the Council after twenty-four years in Indonesia." He smiled. He was neither proud nor apologetic. He obviously was just what he was.

"I thought," he said, "you might want to draw some of the bishops we have in the house here. So I asked them. I am no artist, of course, but you know, I think some of them have quite interesting faces."

Bishop Jan Klooster

"Your Excellency," I began, "I am most grateful that you took all this trouble and—"

"Why don't you call me Jan," he said, again very quietly. "After all, we are a bit related. If you want to, you can draw Monsignor Descuffi, the Archbishop of Smyrna, and I have also asked Monsignor Botéro Salazar of Colombia, and perhaps the Archbishop of Djakarta, Sugijapranata, and the Archbishop of Bandung, Djajasaputra. They are real Indonesians. I am just a naturalized one. You see, I became Indonesian in order to continue my work after I got out of a Japanese concentration camp."

"Let me start with you, Monsignor Jan," I suggested.

He smiled his shy smile.

"Oh, no, not me!" He waved his hands at me in horror. "Oh, no. That would be a wrong start! Who am I anyway? I have no face to draw! I just have a commonplace mug.—I have really been worried what to do for you. This morning in St. Peter's during the session I caught myself looking around for more models for you. If you want, I can get the Coptic Patriarch of Alexandria: you know, he is the one who wears a crown, and the Metropolitan of Latakia, the Greek-Catholic Bishop of Latakia in Syria—I have already asked them. I told everybody you were a famous artist from America, so they said okay! I'll see who else I can drum up for you."

So I was going to draw individual Council Fathers (as the bishops were called here). I had never thought of that. I had come with vague ideas of drawing at press conferences, in St. Peter's Square, perhaps at public sessions of the Council. But Bishop Jan Klooster had given me an excellent idea and a very practical start. I was going to draw the Council from life!

"By the way, you are staying at a hotel, aren't you? I thought that might become very expensive for you. I spoke to the ladies of Casa Unitas and if you want they'll give you a room. It is so much cheaper, and I thought it might be more interesting for you. Actually, it is a hostel for non-Catholic pilgrims and visitors to Rome. It is run by Dutch nuns, the Ladies of Bethany. During the Council some Protestant observers and some of our theologians are living there. You might want to draw them, too."

A few weeks later, while Bishop Jan told about his poverty-stricken Indonesians and spoke about his having been away too long from his diocese, I drew his "commonplace mug." He was now used to me.

My new home was on the fourth floor of an ancient building on the Via dell'Anima, just behind the Piazza Navona, perhaps Rome's most beautiful and intimate square, graced by three monumental fountains, sidewalk cafés serving glorious ice cream, and the most charming of Christmas fairs. A vaulted black-and-white tiled hallway led into the building past a cobblestone courtyard dominated by the dome of the Church of Sant'Agnese. The sound of water came from a spring in one corner. There was a surprisingly modern but tiny elevator, just big enough for me and the fat monsignor who shared it with me—his jowled face as purple as his dicky. I was received by a charming, slim woman of forty in a chic mauve blouse of raw silk. She had springy gray hair and wore a fine piece of silver jewelry. Another artist-guest, I thought. She showed me to my clean, modern room and opened the window.

"I thought this was a convent!"

"It is." She smiled.

"But where are the nuns?"

"Well, I am one of them." A lively woman of about fifty in high heels then appeared in the doorway, both hands outstretched in welcome. "And this is our Mother Superior, Miss Huf."

"I am sorry, ladies, I don't quite understand. Are you really nuns?"

"Yes we are," said Miss Huf, "but we don't wear the habit. Have you never heard of our order? We even have a house in Pittsburgh! You probably know Bishop Wright? He really helped us tremendously."

From the hall I looked down on the Piazza Navona. Children were playing around the fountains, balloon salesmen with their enormous bunches of gigantic multicolored grapes were doing a good business. Couples sat on stone benches licking ices. It had stopped raining. The evening sky was a deep rusty pink now, and innumerable swallows swept through it in their eternal choreography. From my window I saw the rust-colored sky envelop the old city. Red-tiled roofs stretched into the distance, with the dome of St. Peter's in the middle of this roofscape. Bells were ringing from towers all around. The swallows continued their ballet, and the radio tower of Radio Vaticano blinked its red eye rhythmically in the dusk.

I felt as if I were looking straight into the room where the old Pope was now at his desk. I imagined him talking to Cardinal Ottaviani. "Ottaviani," he once said of the most formidable secretary of the Most Sacred Congregation of the Holy Office, "Ottaviani—he is like a child."

I saw Pope John the next morning for the first time. St. Peter's Square was not particularly crowded. Again it was raining. But the window opened at noon, and the small figure appeared, prayed, and blessed the crowd. The figure did not move me; the scene was too much like the movies I had seen.

It was a bit like a first visit to New York. You had seen those skyscrapers so often on film and in photos that you were immunized against surprise. The Empire State Building seemed small in comparison to your expectation. What you had not expected, however, was the tone of voice of your taxi driver, of the policeman from whom you asked directions. These voices brought the realization of actually being in New York. Here, too, it was the voice that woke me. It came reverberating over loudspeakers, incongruous with the small portly figure in the window, gesticulating like a puppet in a

Punch-and-Judy show. It was a warm, vigorous voice, a little raw. This, then, was the voice that had spoken to me while I walked up Fifth Avenue reading the account of his opening speech, and that had called me to Rome.

"Benedictio Dei omnipotentis, Patris et Filii et Spiritus Sancti," the voice ended, blessing the people all around me.

I walked away from the Piazza, a little moved and deadly afraid. What had I undertaken? Why was I here? I sat down in a *caffè-espresso* close to the Vatican. People who had been blessed together with me a few moments ago pushed themselves into the tiny space like stampeding animals, elbowing their way to get their espresso first. They belonged here; they were born to all this; it was their folklore. I felt very strange, and yet at home, foolish and hopeless about the task I had set myself. I felt as if I had come to a country I only knew from dreams. I looked at the compact mass of people and at the rain outside and heard the raw, vital voice again, and I was suddenly filled with astonishment at having survived half a century of utter folly and incredible cruelty, war and constant threats of war, massacre following mass murder, and that I was here now.

You, Pope John, had contradicted Nietzsche's discovery which later became a commonplace. "God is *not* dead," you proclaimed. You knew that *homo religiosus* exists, as he always has. During your eighty years you had watched him searching blindly among political utopias that promised justice and love at the price of cruelty and slavery. You had watched him following in despair pseudo religions and psychological credos, rummaging in Oriental philosophies, adopting fitfully ill-digested techniques of self-transcendence, seeking fulfillment in self-indulgence, comfort, art and pseudo art, music and pseudo music.

Not God is dead, you cried, but the rigid vocabularies of established religion have been allowed to petrify His image in our hearts! The values contained in the ancient Scriptures have not been translated into meaningful concepts for our time, thus causing their general rejection; what once was living water is now stagnant and fetid. You had seen how man's roads to self-transcendence had been blocked by archaisms. You had seen contemporary man wandering in his existential vacuum—contemporary man, who had developed an allergy for stereotyped religious formulations, for obsolete forms of

. . . the bishops started to arrive

the guards, humbly and always unsuccessfully, to let them through.

Then the bishops started to arrive for the nine o'clock session. They arrived by the busload, thirty or forty to a bus marked Nordland Hotel or Albergo Medici. Out they clambered, purple socks and heavy shoes with purple heels first. Purple cassocks followed with all the lace coming next, in disarray over paunches, pectoral crosses dangling. Then more purple socks and after the lace and the gold chains and the crosses more purple socks, until the busload of florid and rotund or ascetic and yellow faces had emptied. Orientals arrived, black- or white-bearded, with the high cylindrical headdress of the Oriental prelates, inheritance from Byzantium. Suddenly the Colonnade was full of bishops—some solemn in their purple, like sinister Richelieus; some obese and jolly; some sour with sharp, middle-aged lawyers' faces; some very old and feeble, hardly able to move on their canes, or spare and emaciated, with eyes that saw visions. They all ran, stepped, shuffled, to the newspaper vendors to get *Le Monde, La Croix,* or *Der Spiegel,* to fill them in on what the cagey *Osservatore Romano* left out and to understand a little better what was going on inside their own sessions in a Babel of Latins: Genoa Latin, German Latin, are, alas, so excruciatingly different from Brooklyn Latin, or Boston Latin, or even Parisian Latin. . . .

It was icy cold. I was sitting at the foot of a column and was sketching, as I so often would have to, with frozen fingers. Now and then a purple figure would stop and glance at my paper with an apologetic smile, that smile people put on when you catch them reading the letter you forgot to take off your desk. I was helped by the fact that my presbyopic eye, in order to see in the distance and at the same time on my paper, worked best with a monocle, and this three-dollar device has saved me from much interference. A stare through a monocle seems to frighten bishops, chamberlains, and even Rolls-Royce owners! It has saved my drawing many a time.

By five minutes to nine some two thousand bishops had sauntered by, followed by the monks and priests with heavy briefcases who were their *periti,* experts in theology, canon law, liturgy. The Square was no longer visible from where I was sitting. It seemed crammed with buses. But at the steps of St. Peter's, limousines were unloading cardinals. They never came by bus, but wore their Mercedes-Benzes with as much ease as their scarlet birettas. By now bishops no longer frightened me. After all, they were delivered by the busload. But I was still awed at the thought of having to draw cardinals.

As the big bells of the Basilica struck nine, the Square was empty. The purple mass, dotted with the black and brown habits of Dominicans, Franciscans, and Capuchins, had climbed the steps, some quickly, some painfully. The Council was in session; the Mass had started.

To get warm I fled to one of those little espresso bars on the Via della Conciliazione, the ornamental mall that leads from St. Peter's to the Tiber and the ancient Castel San Angelo. The corrosive coffee and the miserable Roman sandwiches—consisting of a hot-dog roll split open, smeared with Mobil-oily mayonnaise and garnished with three dime-slim slices of cold frankfurter—increased my melancholia. All I could do now was wait for what the press had so lyrically termed the "purple waterfall"—the supposedly riotous action and color of the bishops descending the steps at the close of the morning sessions. It was raining again. At twelve-thirty the purple waterfall took shape. I stood shivering in the shelter of the Colonnade, sketchbook at the ready; gusts of wind blew water in to my face and made the ink run. I was not drawing, I was doing Japanese sumi, New York School action painting. Every stroke dribbled, splattered, and ran. Even the bishops, as far and as fast as their not-so-young legs could carry them, ran to their buses. "Purple waterfall" indeed! Two thousand old men in wet, faded, magenta evening dresses, rushing out of a super-movie palace to catch a bus, I thought bitterly, as the secret and not-so-secret police chased me all too literally from pillar to post.

There were the two very old bishops whom I was to see day after day, shuffling down the steps, supporting each other on their arthritic legs. They were streaming with water. Nobody seemed to care. At the bottom of the steps the bus was waiting for them, and the lesser invalid gently lifted the legs of his colleague one by one onto the high step of the bus. Only once during my stay did I see a private car take pity on the two venerable ancients. Their expression of surprised gratitude was more moving than all the purple waterfalls taken together.

The morning session over, the Basilica was open to the public. I was allowed to gape with the tourists at the purple-and-gold grandstands that filled the enormous church, transforming it into a huge

and stuffy theater-in-the-round. A plainclothesman spotted me immediately and confiscated my sketchbook. Sketchbooks obviously were
regarded as potentially explosive. I withdrew to the espresso-cum-
jukebox.

How could I have been so stupid, such an irresponsible imbecile

...the morning session over

as to drop my work in New York and take it for granted that anything could have happened to me in Rome other than standing in
the cold rain, looking at "purple waterfalls." As if Rome would bow

down, so glad that at last, at last, Frederick Franck had deigned to come and draw the Ecumenical Council! Had I perhaps expected to see Pope John, standing at the third window from the right in the Apostolic Palace, nudge Cardinal Ottaviani: "Look, Alfredo, isn't that something? There is Franck with his sketchbook near the obelisk! Run down and bring him up, Alfredo. Quick, Your Eminence, before he is off again."

The next espresso seemed to bore through the stomach lining and woke me from my bitter reverie. The jukebox had stopped. It was quiet; above the din of the scooters and the rain, the bells of St. Peter's struck two. Hopelessly I took out my notebook and two forgotten cards fell out. They were the ones given me by my Dutch friend, the Baron-Burgomaster, who is also a secret Chamberlain Extraordinary of the Sword and Cloak to His Holiness. I believe that this entitles him to take people to their places in St. Peter's on very solemn occasions, an usher with a ruffled collar and a fine sword.

One card was addressed: "His Excellency Petrus Canisius van Lierde, Sagrista et Vicario Generale de Sua Santità, Città del Vaticano." The other card was for Brother Welsh in the Anticamera. Both cards begged assistance for me.

I'll go there tomorrow, I thought.

Another espresso. But tomorrow I would have to go back to Bishop Klooster and draw his bishops. Tonight a lecture at Casa Unitas was scheduled. Already two days were lost. I'd better go right now! At the Vatican, the *gendarmeria* stopped me lazily, where it had stopped me in the morning. I showed the card "His Excellency," etc. The gendarme saluted. *"Portone di Bronzo,"* he pointed out politely. I walked on to the Bronze Door. There I showed the card to the Swiss guards. The blond, pimply one took his halberd out of my way and pointed to an older Swiss guard, behind a little desk, who was picking his teeth with a pencil. He spoke French and told me the way to Brother Welsh. (At the last moment I had thought it wiser to start with a brother before tackling an archbishop.) Proudly I walked up the endless, steep stone stairs of the Vatican. Although it was but the prelude to an initiation, it felt like an acceptance. On the left, the door to Brother Welsh stood open. A man in livery, like a bank guard without gun, brought me to the brother's desk and showed him my card as introduction.

"Well, well, dear Baron." Brother Welsh got up to his full length and huge bulk and his voice brogued like the roaring of the Liffey. "Long time no see! And how are you and the Missus Baroness?"

Brother Welsh did not change a bit after the slight mix-up was corrected. He was just as delighted. He promised me some very fine tickets to the public sessions of the Council; he gave me most valuable pointers; he invited me to tea in the reception room of his convent; and my only faux pas was when I inquired whether the three sisters Brother Welsh spoke about so feelingly, his three sisters in Australia, had grown-up children. "Oh, no, indeed not," roared Brother Welsh, "they are all three Reverend Mothers."

He had been making appointments for audiences and distributing tickets for ceremonies and blessed medals to newlyweds for over twenty years. But what a change had come to the Vatican with Pope John! During the papacy of Pius XII, Brother Welsh said, the Pope had never even noticed him. The only contact he could remember was a note he had written to the Holy Father announcing the audience of an important member of the Augustinian order. "I had written '*A*gustinian,' that is the way we pronounce it in Ireland, and it came back to me with the word struck out and corrected in red ink by the Pope himself, like in school.

"Well, Pope John had been crowned only a few days and here he walks into this here office. 'You are Father Welsh, I guess,' he said. 'I am *Brother* Welsh, Your Holiness,' I replied. 'So you are *Mr.* Welsh,' said Pope John, 'I thought you were a priest.' 'No, I am a Christian Brother,' I said. So the Pope gave me a big smile and he says: 'No Father, no Mister, no fish, no fowl.' When he was carried the first time in the *sedia gestatoria* he said to the bearers: 'How much did Pacelli weigh?' Answer: 'About 120 pounds, Your Holiness.' 'And how much do you earn?' '16,000 lire, Your Holiness.' 'All right, then, it is no more than just that you earn 32,000 lire from now on. Twice the work, twice the pay.' "

Brother Welsh could not stop the anecdotes about the hero we had in common. "There was an audience here a few weeks ago," he said, "and six generals and admirals were presented to the Pope with all their beautiful titles and hyphenated names, and when it had all stopped, good Pope John gets up from his throne with that smile of his, and he stands to attention and salutes and says: 'Sergente Roncalli.' "

I left the Vatican with a distinct feeling of belonging.

[39]

Cardinals' limousines leaving St. Peter's

Next day, in the dank, hollow Casa della Missione, Giuseppe Descuffi, Archbishop of Smyrna and Izmir, was waiting for me on the third floor. At the top of the dismal stone staircase, I turned to the right through long corridors that smelled acrid, like a hospital no longer in use. There was a wait after my knock. A very old patriarchal man with a square white beard, thin as a wraith, opened the door. He limped slowly and painfully, "I broke my hip a few months ago," he explained. "I am most flattered that you think me worthy of being sketched," he went on, offering me a chair which he insisted on pulling with great effort closer to the table that served as a desk. "Are you sure you are comfortable there? I am sorry our furniture is not more luxurious."

The long, dark room was cheerless and quite empty. On a floor of waxed planks stood the narrow bed with a St. Sulpice crucifix over it; there was the one straight plush armchair with clangy springs on which I was sitting. The wardrobe door stood ajar as if it could not close properly. On the table near the window a chaos of books, pamphlets, and papers. The Latin proceedings of the Council lay open.

"What do you prefer me to do?" the old man asked with exquisite politeness of tone and gesture. He spoke a very elegant French. He actually looked like an ancient French duke, mid-nineteenth century, elected a member of the French Academy in recognition of a distinguished work in history or entomology. But he told me he was an Italian, born in Turkey seventy years ago.

"I don't want to disturb Your Excellency at all," I said in what was to become my stock phrase with the prelates. "Please continue whatever you were doing." The old man coughed a long, hoarse cough. "I hope it is not too cold for you in this room," he murmured. "I'll go on, then, preparing my statement to the Council for tomorrow." His eyes were very deep-set. He had taken up his pen again and prepared himself to continue writing his statement. To warm up I started to scribble a first sketch. There was a knock. "Oh, how unfortunate that I have to interrupt you," the old archbishop apologized. He limped to the door, gesturing that I should remain seated. A little, plump peasant girl loaded with shirts and clean sheets came in. He bowed to her as though she were a princess. "Just put it on the bed, my dear," he said, holding the door to show her out again. "Merci infiniment, ma chère fille." He bowed, closing the door behind her.

Drawing the Archbishop of Smyrna and Izmir I drew a legendary period in history closed forever, a period of formality not yet petrified into empty good manners, a formality that still conveyed a spiritual message, where "Good morning" meant quite consciously both a wish and a statement about the goodness of mornings. In drawing Descuffi, as my pen followed the line of the eyebrows, the deep hollows above the eyes, the strong finely built nose, I saw what Rembrandt may have seen when he drew his old rabbis: a wisdom attained, inseparable from gentleness and compassion, a compassion that expressed itself in a most sensitive courtesy. He made the cheerless room glow with his accomplished humanity. He wrote, and over his glasses studied the Latin documents. He talked a bit about his life and he went on writing. All at once he seemed to bend over and the pen slipped out of his hand. I felt a sudden anxiety. But the old archbishop had just dozed off. After a few minutes he woke up just as suddenly. He glanced at me as if he hoped I had not noticed and went on writing. He insisted afterward on limping with me through the long dingy hallways to the room of Archbishop Botéro Salazar of Medellín, Colombia, and on introducing me.

The room of the Latin American prelate was not lighter, but more luxurious, with gleaming old-fashioned mahogany furniture, a more ornamental bed, and a real desk. The face of the man gave me an initial shock. After the finesse of Descuffi, this was a standard ecclesiastical head; it was nearly a caricature of one particular type of churchly face one finds everywhere in the world: rather heavy, a little too snub-nosed cherubic to harmonize with the jowls, with rimless glasses and quite wakeful eyes in an easy, professional half-smile behind them. Cardinal Spellman is America's most distinguished wearer of this priestly face.

Archbishop Salazar, too, asked me what I wanted him to do. I answered with my standard phrase of not wishing to disturb. This allowed the face to show its natural preoccupation. Anyway, no one can assume a pose for twenty minutes and pretend to what he is not. While being photographed, one can assume a pose, an expression of profundity, goodwill, energetic decisiveness. The photographer with a miniature camera will give you a choice from among the dozens of pictures he shoots. A few poses are certain to flatter the sitter by

Archbishop Giuseppe Descuffi of Smyrna

confirming his favorite self-image. But while being drawn or painted, the smile soon vanishes or hardens into a grimace, the energetically closed lips relax, the hand falls limp on the table, and the man becomes what he is, an all too mortal thing, moved by rather than moving the universe. And with this mortal thing, I can communicate and usually identify, as I start my first scribble to make the acquaintance. At the end I may ask for a few minutes of "posing," but only after I have been able to absorb and identify with the face before me.

Archbishop Salazar had been reading his breviary. "Do you mind if I go on praying?" he asked. "Please move wherever you like." He folded his hands and prayed. His fingers were pale and knobby. The stone of his ring caught the dusky light. He seemed to have forgotten me completely, or rather he was aware of my presence, but another Presence had taken over. I watched him passionately as I drew. This was no pose. The cherublike face had lost its smile, the eyes were half-closed, the breviary reflected a little light onto the double chin. He was motionless; only the lips moved, hardly visibly. All caricature had vanished from his face, which became noble, human, and beautiful. I could not stop drawing this revelation—four, five, six times. We had hardly exchanged a word when I noticed the room had become quite dark. We shook hands and thanked one another warmly and gravely. I later heard that Monsignor Botéro Salazar was the archbishop who had given away his palace, so that it could be used as a hospital for the poor.

Not always is prayer so intense and inward as with Botéro Salazar: I had an appointment to draw a Curia bishop. He lived in one of those palaces outside the walls of the Vatican where you wait in a dull waiting room; faded curtains of what was once gold moiré had turned into joyless yellow; on a console a marble bust of Pius X stood smiling inanely in what a poor sculptor took for sanctity; on the walls some oil portraits of cardinals wrapped in hack-painted scarlet splendor. There were six gilt chairs with throne pretensions. An ornamental doorway of dark walnut bore a coat of arms and was flanked by two enormous Renaissance candlesticks that ended in electric bulbs.

Archbishop Botéro Salazar

The bishop kept me waiting. At last a tall, thickset man with heavy features and a bulbous nose shuffled into the room. His skin was a too florid network of tiny purple veins. I could hear his doctor say: "You will have to lose weight, Your Excellency!" His gestures were a mixture of elaborately ceremonial politeness, condescension, and distrust; his English was Italianate but very correct.

"Where do you want to draw me?" he asked. "Here, or behind my desk?" "Maybe behind your desk. I would prefer you to work or read as usual." He went before me into his study and started to clear his desk. "Not necessary, Your Excellency, not at all. I leave all that out anyway." "Oh, no, dear sir, I can't stand this mess while you are drawing me." "I just want you to be yourself, Your Excellency, and read or work." "I'll say my prayers if you don't mind," he said a little sharply. "Of course, Your Excellency, as you wish." "Well, you see, I have to. I am not through for the day. Are you comfortable in that chair?" "Yes, indeed, I am, thank you," I said, wiping away the first drops of sweat. "Are you sure? I can give you another chair. With pleasure."

The prayer book was lying in front of him. He pulled a precious ornamental crucifix closer and folded his hands, fixing the ring so that its fine stone reflected the light from the desk lamp. I had started my warming-up scribble. "I am sorry, but I really must pray," he started again in his very precise English. "There are certain prayers which— Can you see me well this way?" "Excellent," I said, "perfect." "Or rather this way," he went on, as if he had not heard me, keeping his hands folded but turning his face a little toward me, and then away again, eyeing the ceiling. I did not reply, but scribbled a second sketch. What was getting on my paper looked horrifying. Fingers can be tongue-tied too. The sweat was dripping. "You are sure this is the right angle," His Excellency asked, looking up from his prayer book, "and that you are perfectly comfortable? Make yourself completely at home, dear sir." "Of course, Your Excellency." I tore off a new sheet and started again. I too was praying now.

"I'll finish my prayers quite soon, then I can do something else," the Bishop said reassuringly. "Oh, no," I said, and though I could not imagine my expression I did not like my tone of voice, "there is nothing more inspiring to draw than a man in communication with his God." The Bishop kept his pose this time, but he turned his eyes toward me under his long eyelids and gave me a strange, poisonous look. "May I see what you have been doing?" he asked when at last I gave up.

"Oh," I said, using one of those unblinking lies I have practiced to perfection, "these are only the notes I take on the spot. At home I work them out and make a synthesis." This lets me off the hook of criticism. For although in the past there have been numerous princes of the Church who were patrons of the arts, their successors, judging by the ecclesiastical interior decoration of contemporary Rome, must have completely lost interest in the arts a few hundred years ago. Hence I prefer to exercise that virtue nowhere praised so much as it is in Catholic Rome, that archaic, precious virtue called "prudentia." "I shall send you a photostat of it," I promised.

"Are you sure you have all you need now?" he inquired with something like anxiety in his voice.

"If it is not too much to ask, I'd like to do one quick sketch in the reception room."

I placed him on one of the thrones next to one of the gigantic candlesticks. He sat down and looked regal. Now I felt in my element and started to enjoy myself. It took longer than either he or I had expected: that candlestick was fascinating and complicated. Every now and then I saw the old bishop nod. He closed his eyes and slumped.

"Hi, Excellency!" I cried. He opened his eyes and reassumed his kingly pose, looking down at me once more from his ecclesiastical Olympus.

Back in New York I carefully chose the two sketches in which he looked almost human, had them photostated, and sent them off. The Bishop thanked me in English; he wrote:

"Will you allow me just to express a judgment? It is that I think both pictures good, and true. Only, the underlip, and the part of the face under the lips, is not pleasing as it is. I find that the expression has the effect of being somewhat moody, unsatisfied, tired, or lacking in serenity—I mean only from this part of the face as it results. If you could take this out I should be happy and pleased. This is my humble opinion, as regards an effect which strikes me in your beautiful work. With my sincere gratitude and admiration. . . ."

My appointment to draw Archbishop Peter Canisius van Lierde was for 9:00 A.M. His function as Sagrista is a complex one, but only in exceptional circumstances does it become hectic. He is the liturgical assistant to the Pope during ceremonies in St. Peter's. A few months later the Archbishop's photograph was to appear in the world's press after he had brought the last sacrament to the dying Pope John. But it was now early December and the illness the Pope was suffering from had not yet been disclosed, even under such euphemistic terms as anemia or stomach disorder.

The Archbishop lives in the very bowels of the Vatican, and one needs a pass to penetrate there. At the Bronze Door the Swiss guard sends the visitor to his lieutenant and the lieutenant points to the dark *loge de concierge,* where three men are at work giving out passes. There is a questionnaire to be filled out: Whom do you want to see? On

. . . to draw a Curia bishop

what subject? Where were you born? Married or single? (There is no column for divorced.) I was told that the questionnaire had been simplified recently as a concession to these informal times. Also, it is now in Italian instead of Latin.

In the gloomy cubicle three dyspeptic-looking men sat under the light of a bare bulb. The visitors filling out questionnaires were middle-aged women in black, who whispered advice to one another while filling out the blue and yellow slips, then brought them on tiptoe to the wan men behind the window. All three wore expressions of utter contempt above well-worn jackets. They glanced at the slips, pointed out a mistake or omission, lazily phoned the dignitary concerned, taking on precisely adjusted attitudes of deference, then gave their verdict, again in tones of brusque contempt.

My archbishop could not keep our appointment. He spoke to me on the phone. "The Holy Father suddenly needed me. I am awfully sorry. Could you make it tonight, perhaps at six thirty?"

At six fifteen that evening I entered the Portone di Bronzo once more in my black coat, my black hat, my black suit, carrying the large, black drawing portfolio. The Swiss guard knew me by now. The big leather portfolio, in combination with my near ecclesiastical attire, looked portentous instead of bohemian. I always hoped that it gave the impression that I was carrying huge secret documents written on parchment for posterity. The men in the *loge* had gone home to their fat wives by now. The sergeant of the Swiss guards looked sleepy. "Just go ahead," he yawned. "How do I find Monsignor van Lierde?" I asked. "Go up the *Scala Regia*, turn right. There is a bell in the *Sala Ducale* with his name on it. Then go up the little staircase on your left." I started to walk up the huge stone stairway. It seemed endless and I got out of breath. Bearers had carried popes innumerable times up and down this Royal Staircase, but I had to walk and drag my portfolio; there was less and less light. Where I had to turn right, the stairs became completely dark. There was not a soul around. At the top I pushed aside the heavy velvet curtain and entered the huge hall, where a tiny bulb was glowing. There were six great ornamental doors. I tried the first one on my left. It was locked. I tried the second one. It had no nameplate. On my right I moved the leaden velvet curtain away; the door behind it was not locked and as I pushed I found myself in a dark lavatory.

Another door gave way and I stood in a chapel where a single priest was in deep prayer. I turned around and tiptoed out. The fourth door had something like a bellpull hanging next to it. I pulled it timidly a few times. No reply. Then I gave it a very energetic pull; the heavy curtain came shut and hit me in the face. The next door opened and I found myself in fresh air in a dimly lit courtyard. The taillight of a big car was visible. "Hello," I cried, "could you tell me—" At that moment the car pulled away. I looked at my watch. It was close to a quarter to seven. My shout had warned someone and a window opened. "I can't find Archbishop van Lierde's bell," I cried out, nearly weeping with rage. "It is in the *Sala Ducale*, first door on your left," a young voice answered pleasantly. "I know, but I can't find it!" A young priest came downstairs, crossed the courtyard, and took me to the Archbishop's door. It really existed; this was no Kafka dream. The hall I had been in was the one next to the *Sala Ducale!*

The priest who opened the door told me to wait a few minutes in the dingy little hallway. Two Roman archbishop hats with green tassels were hanging on a hook above heaps of books and officially stamped papers. I was relieved and euphoric now; as I was trying on one of the hats I heard the creaking of a door. I just had time to put on my official face: "Your Excellency, forgive me, I am late. I lost my way." He was about fifty, tall and fleshy, a face gone heavy in which the boy was still visible. He spoke Dutch with precision, but with a Flemish accent that seemed to make it deliberately quaint and archaic. He was very polite, but it was a cold politeness. Had he caught me in his hat, after all? I had the impression he was afraid to seem too informally friendly. We first sat down on little gilt chairs in his anteroom. I had felt that here I had to bring a present, a copy of my *Days with Albert Schweitzer*. He looked at the book and into it. "Is it medical?" he asked after a few moments. "No," I said, "not at all, but I worked with Dr. Schweitzer and I thought this might interest you. It also shows you some of my drawings." "Aha," he said, looking at the book with an uncomprehending stare. "Who is this Dr. Schweitzer, anyhow?" he asked a little suspiciously. "*The* Dr. Schweitzer, Your Excellency." Had he really never heard of him? I told him about my work in Lambaréné and then about Schweitzer's Nobel Prize. "Aha," he said again. "Of course, of course. Indeed."

Before leaving New York I had asked my publishers, my gallery, and the head of a Catholic publishing house to give me letters of recommendation. Nobody believed they would do me any good, but I took them just in case. Roman newspapermen confirmed this evaluation of my glowing letters. One suggested, "Get yourself a press card anyway. It is no help at all, but who knows?" I applied for it and the press officer, Monsignor Fausto Valainc, graciously issued Permesso No. 1409, affixed my photograph, and certified that I represented a newspaper. I proudly pocketed the elegant little passport bound in blue leather and embossed in gold with the papal arms.

I waved it at the gendarmes when I entered St. Peter's; I waved it at noble and less noble guards at ceremonies, at ruffle-collared chamberlains with and without sword and cloak—and learned that one could not wave anything more offensive at these men. They always waved "No," or they stuck up their thumb and pumped it over their shoulder: "Vìa!"—"Vanish!"

Why did the Vatican waste money on these handsome booklets? The man of the London *Times* told me dryly: "It empowers you to use the nonexistent press facilities." The fellow from the Cleveland *Plain Dealer* put it succinctly: "It gives you free use of the men's room in the Ufficio Stampa, but it is always 'occupato.'" Actually, one could walk into the Stampa for basic needs without any identification. Everyone walked in to look at the daily replenished display of photographs of Council Fathers, smiling into the cameras of the monopoly photographers.

I studied these photographs systematically, looking for good subjects. The shabby young men who snapped them in the mornings and took orders for them in the afternoons had begun to know me. I assumed that they had been chosen for their piety, for the photographs were commonplace.

"Who is this impressive-looking cardinal?" I asked one of them.

"That is Ruffini, the old devil!" he spat. "Your American bishops are all right. They talk to you like human beings. The Dutch are okay, the Germans, too." His Adam's apple was jumping angrily in his scrawny neck. "The Italians, they think they are kings. They treat you like dirt. Look at those faces!" He slapped the faces of a group of Italian cardinals with the heel of his hand. "Phooey!"

"Mangiapreti!" ("priest-eater") his fatter colleague mocked him in a sarcastic whisper, pretending to devour a photograph and rubbing his stomach. "But not this one: he is too thin, that old Scotch gander." An ascetic, fanatic face stared out of the photograph. I had identified Cardinal Heard.

The only day I could have used my press pass I had left it in another suit. It was the day Professor Oscar Cullmann spoke to the press. Cullmann, the most influential Protestant at the Council, is a world-famous New Testament scholar, who holds simultaneous professorships at the Sorbonne and at the University of Basel. His relationship with the Vatican are excellent and he might be nicknamed Mr. Separated Brother. He was at the Council officially as a guest of the Secretariat for the Promotion of Christian Unity; unofficially he acted as the minister plenipotentiary for the non-Catholic observers. Half an hour before he spoke the press office was crowded with bishops and theologians. Suddenly press cards had to be produced.

Father John B. Sheerin, editor of the New York monthly magazine *Catholic World,* tried to smuggle me in on his card, but I was turned away. At that moment an American priest slapped Father Sheerin

the press room

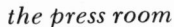

Professor Oscar Cullmann

on the shoulder. He was a square man, white-wirehaired, with a big round head and intense light-blue eyes that popped out when he spoke: "I just can't stand people who don't know their way around! Come on, young fellow." I followed my new guide, who ran up the stairs two steps at a time, pulling up his rather greasy cassock, while asking questions breathlessly. He ran across a few landings on the third floor, as I tried to keep up with him, answering his questions, out of breath and dragging my portfolio. Then he started rushing down another staircase, across another landing, and suddenly we were in the middle of the guarded conference room. He still found time to push me onto a chair in the middle of a pride of bishops, fish for his card in his cassock, and shout "Call me tomorrow around ten" as he pushed it at me. When I regained my breath, I read the card: "Father Francis Xavier Murphy, Professor of Patristic Theology, Academia Alfonsiana, Via Merulana, Roma." The bishops looked with some amazement at the man with the sketchbook suddenly in their midst, and those nearby divided their attention between Professor Cullmann in person and the Cullmann that began to appear on my paper.

Professor Cullmann, who is an Alsatian, spoke flawless, clipped French. I thought at first he looked arrogant. As he spoke his head was tilted backward, the eyes half-closed behind his gleaming glasses.

He expressed the gratitude of all the Protestant observers at the

Council for the honors paid them as representatives of non-Catholic Christians, and for their unprecedented freedom to attend all the secret proceedings of the Council.

Later I was to meet Professor Cullmann often. What I had so carelessly mistaken for arrogance was actually caused by an eye condition that forced him to peer from under half-closed eyelids through thick glasses. He proved to be a man of the most enlightened tolerance, humor, and modesty. It was Professor Cullmann who later, when I drew him in his room, was to show me a charming personal letter written by Cardinal Montini, whose handwriting amazed me: it was not that of a complex intellectual; it was so open, so clear and simple that one would have taken it for that of an orderly schoolboy.

It was also Professor Cullmann who for the last seventeen years had lectured at the Waldensian Seminary in Rome, which had of course been traditionally off-limits for Catholic priests. Slowly, however, Catholic theologians had begun to attend Cullmann's lectures, and an atmosphere of mutual appreciation had gradually developed where once reigned an almost bloodthirsty hatred. Professor Cullmann had been one of those who, unbeknownst to themselves, had prepared the ground for this Ecumenical Council.

"When years ago Father Yves Congar came to visit me in Strasbourg, our little maid burst into my room, utterly horrified, as if she had seen Satan. 'Herr Professor, there is a Catholic priest outside. He wants to come in!' Much has changed. We all have regular contact now."

At this gathering there was one face that fascinated me even more than that of the speaker. It was a very old, very sweet and saintly face, framed by nearly white wisps of hair and crowned with the headdress of an Oriental prelate. "Qui est ça?" I whispered to the bishop next to me, who was following every line I put on paper. "C'est Monseigneur Cassien, recteur du Seminaire Russe Orthodoxe de Paris, invité du Secretariat," he whispered back.

I called Father Murphy next morning, and drew him in his room at the Academia Alfonsiana, a room that reminded me of our maid's room in my youth, complete with iron bedstead and rickety table. But it was full of books and magazines, and smelled of printed paper, which lay in heaps barring the way, wherever one went. When Father Murphy wanted to show me a paper he had just published, he pulled it from under the heap on his bed. While I was drawing him, he talked excitedly—this man seemed to be constantly excited—about the Council and how it was going in the right direction.

I asked him what he thought of the amazingly well-informed "Letters from Vatican City" that were appearing in *The New Yorker* over the signature "Xavier Rynne." "Pretty good," he said.

"Who wrote them, do you know?" I asked. "Everybody is asking who could possibly have written them."

"Oh," Father Murphy laughed, showing all his prominent pipe-smoker's teeth, "there are rumors that it was written by a group of priests under a pseudonym." And he very quickly changed the subject to talk about when he was a U.S. Army chaplain in Korea and Chief Army Chaplain in Berlin.

"Are you a New Yorker, Father?"

"And how!" he said with a big Fernandel grin. "My dad was a cop in the Bronx! By the way, if you want to draw some of the Redemptorist bishops who are staying here, you're welcome—or perhaps Father Häring? I could get you Archbishop Hermaniuk of Winnipeg too. He's from the Ukrainian rite and he is our guest."

Archbishop Hermaniuk, his moujik face earnest under the Ukrainian biretta, was having a discussion with Redemptorist theologians. I was concentrating on my drawing and could not follow the conversation closely, but it was clear that here too the spirit was "progressive." Wherever I went, I heard progressive sounds in the air. The use of the terms "progressive" or "liberal" versus "conservative" or "traditional" to denote, respectively, the forward-looking and backward-looking attitudes at the Council has been severely criticized as being misleading. And they are, insofar as they are borrowed from, and easily confused with, political stereotypes. Many synonyms have been suggested for the two basic attitudes displayed by the bishops at the Council, attitudes of open-mindedness versus closed-mindedness, of dynamism versus staticism.

One misunderstands the mood of the Council and the issues at stake completely if one sees a battle between good guys and bad guys or assumes that the open-minded theologians and bishops are less orthodox, less passionately Catholic than the closed-minded ones, however much they may differ in theology and methodology. In its pure form, the immobile, triumphalistic, authoritarian orthodoxy of the closed-minded group is a frozen orthodoxy that identifies itself with a four-hundred-year-old system of values, of abstract logic,

Msgr. Cassien, Russian-Orthodox of Paris

and of vocabulary, a literally sacrosanct vocabulary within which it feels itself secure and which it believes to be the very essence of Christianity and the Church. It attacks any doubt of the validity of the smallest detail of this system as if it were a malicious assault on the Church. It sees the Church as a juridical society of which it, the frozen orthodoxy, is the sole guardian, as it stands beleaguered amidst its enemies, ever triumphant over the onslaughts of a historical development that it only recognizes sufficiently to condemn. Wherever it has to compromise under intolerable pressure it does so while keeping its abstract vocabulary intact, rationalizing compromises in theological doubletalk, camouflaging even the most dubious *combinaziones* with temporal power by traditionally pious language. How else could the Inquisition and the Concordat with Hitler be made consistent with the Church?

Firmly entrenched in Rome, the frozen orthodox establishment has kept itself deliberately out of contact with that vast majority of humanity that is non-Catholic, ignoring or condemning it. Unable or unwilling to recognize the pluralistic development of contemporary society, it remains defensively on its rampart of *Romanità,* demanding from its faithful absolute and unquestioning loyalty and abject docility to its decrees. Neglecting the great moral issues of our time, it remains obsessed with narrow theological issues and often exclusively sexual moralism. When the pressures of history become too strong, it grudgingly grants peripheral concessions, finds compromise solutions using complex sophistry in order to pretend to itself and the world that its immobile systems of medieval and Renaissance theology and mentality have remained perfectly intact, meanwhile, ironically, dispatching its often archaic directives and condemnations by its own radio transmitters and by jet-airmail across continents and oceans.

The "progressive" group, while being just as faithful to every dogma of the Church, is profoundly convinced that its essential teachings can be made relevant once more to our entire world, but it has observed that the emphasis on the Church as a juridical, tyrannical body instead of a spiritual community is an obsolete and increasingly embarrassing liability, which has caused the defection of important sections of the faithful, hampered the activities of the missions, estranged non-Catholic Christians, and given sharp weapons to those who will decry all religion as an "opium of the people." They recognize the "mass movement of workers and intellectuals away from the Church which has come with industrialized society. We must not act as if we were still in the sixteenth century!" as a German bishop exclaimed in the Council. The "progressives" are mainly those from countries of Western Europe where Catholics have had long experience in living among Proestants and unbelievers, and so have been in contact with the realities of mixed societies. They are well aware that the most valuable attainments of such societies, their democratic institutions, their scientific and technological progress, cannot be credited to the Church. They have learned to see man as he is, living in his historical, sociological, economic, and psychological context. They realize that in order to communicate with him, the comparatively recent traditions of the frozen orthodoxy, born in the still feudal society of the Counter-Reformation, have to be replaced by what is really basic in Catholic teaching.

In this process of soul-searching it became clear that each individual Council Father is within himself an individual mixture of conservative and progressive ingredients. The conservative side of his character was formed at his mother's knee, was molded in the seminary. The progressive component had developed in his contact with the real world he confronted in his work with contemporary people, whether in a parish in Amsterdam or Chicago or a diocese in Indonesia. Insofar as he was conscious of his "progressive" attitude, he often felt guilty, as if he were harboring an inadmissible, private heresy developed in his isolation. At the Council, in intimate contact with his fellows from all over the world, he gradually discovered that he shared his doubts, his problems, and his tentative solutions with a majority of them.

The Roman Curia, on the other hand, protected by its bureaucratic protocol, insulated from the world, had never been confronted with contemporary man in the concrete. In them the "conservative" ingredient continued to dominate. The lessons of the seminary had never been corrected by confrontation with reality. On the contrary: the conformism instilled there combined with ambition were the prerequisites for a successful career. The progressive explosion in the Council was not only a threat to the Roman mentality; it was an inexplicable and perverse spectacle when watched from behind baroque curial desks. Cardinal Frings' formulation, that "the Church founded by Christ is always to be reformed," to which the majority subscribed so eagerly, was a direct menace to its vested interests.

Thus the cynics are wrong to assume that the "progressives" have merely changed tactics. They are influenced by a revivification of the religious spirit characteristic of our time at its best. This revivification has nothing to do with that widely applauded "religious revival" that has resulted in crowded churches, crowded with not necessarily religiously motivated people. Especially in America, churchgoing is a technique of conformism. "Worshiping togetherness" is all too often a social commitment rather than a truly religious one, and membership in a church is often the social equivalent of membership in a country club. Vague religiosity and the cliché-mouthing of the word God by politicians in order to confer respectability on unrespectable undertakings has contributed to the devaluation of religious language. There is hardly a barbaric hate-group that does not, like the Ku Klux Klan, claim the seal of Christianity.

Alfredo Cardinal Ottaviani

In contrast to this idolatrous civic religion, we witness the rebirth in contemporary man of a truly religious preoccupation that has followed the deep disillusionment with the positivism and the materialistic Utopianism of the nineteenth century, and the despair caused by the cataclysms of the twentieth century. In the midst of our self-induced catastrophes, our posterity and our frustration, we are, on the edge of the abyss, engaged in a passionate search for ultimate meaning. Our delving in psychological theories, in ancient myth, in comparative religion, in Oriental mysticism must be seen as part of this renewed religious concern.

Among us, many of the best now shudder at the use of a Christian idiom, abused for centuries, flee the traditional religious establishments, compromised by too frequent identification with a naïve bourgeois optimism, moralism, and activity, by a shocking callousness to social evil and racial injustice, by an absurd tolerance for nationalistic cant and crime.

On the other hand, post-Freudian psychology has shifted to the recognition of an "existential vacuum" basic to modern man's unhappiness and neuroses, and has concerned itself increasingly with problems of self-fulfillment and the "peak experiences" of a non-denominational mysticism that recognizes the limitations of language to express fully the very ultimate meanings and relationships to which it can merely point, but which only our direct intuitions are capable of comprehending.

Having come full circle, we are now beginning to overcome this detestation of the Establishment and begin to suspect that we have thrown out the religious baby with the dirty clerical water.

Under the mountains of rejected remnants and undigested theological theorems, we discern traces of those hidden verities no longer to be found by docile conformism, but to be rediscovered, as by accident, after long and persistent personal quest for wholeness in the face of the increasingly absurd and obscene demands of society.

We are on a pilgrimage to that very Reality, that God, hidden where least expected, hinted at in the archaic words of all Scriptures, Scriptures that yield new meaning when reread with the eyes open for existential rather than historical aspects.

The progressive theologians of the Church are the specifically Catholic manifestations of this revivification, of this new religious spirit and this quest for wholeness. The bishops were stirred by it, more or less, according to their own level of enlightenment and their own openness of spirit. Even so, many of them feared that a too rapid introduction of radical changes might confuse the simple-minded in the more backward areas of the world, as well as those routine Catholics who are neither religiously nor intellectually wide-awake. Yet they realized their profound alliance with those theologians and

Augustin Cardinal Bea, S.J.

liturgists, who, critical of the Establishment and realizing the vanity of mere assent and conformism, had in their total commitment created a resurrection of Catholic awareness relevant to modern man's spiritual needs. They were less obsessed by fear of treason, subversion, and heresy than with the survival of those values that the Church—insofar as it has been true to its mission—has transmitted to its faithful throughout its history. Pope John embodied this renewed and wholly spiritual commitment. And it seemed as though the entire world had been waiting for this Joannine Church, that it was overripe for it.

There was euphoria in the Roman air, an expectancy of great changes, a great happiness and an infectious joy. Pent-up frustrations and criticisms were being aired everywhere. Doubts repressed for years were uttered aloud. The staid old Church exuded a spirit of—eminently loyal—rebelliousness. Wherever one of the open-minded theologians, so long harassed and persecuted by the Holy Office, lectured, enthusiastic multitudes of bishops, priests, and seminarians were on hand to bring long ovations. Fathers Congar, Daniélou, de Lubac, and Küng spoke to overflow audiences and were cheered like champions. Jokes circulating among journalists and Council Fathers had the defenders of the status quo as their butt. They are repeated here not as jokes, but as symptoms of a mental climate.

Father Hans Küng

The Kyrie Eleison of the Mass, I heard in one monastery, was going to be changed into "Curia Eleison." . . . A special prayer—embarrassingly cruel—for Cardinal Ottaviani, who is blind in one eye, was proposed: "Lord, please open the cardinal's blind eye, or else close them both gently."

The possibility was goodhumoredly discussed that apart from the two coffee bars in St. Peter's, nicknamed Bar Jonah and Bar-Abbas, a third would soon be opened, to be called "Bar Mitzvah."

In another monastery I heard one bishop kid another: "Have you seen the sign in the window of the Holy Office? It says 'Store for Rent.' " The second bishop countered: "Do you know why Cardinal Ruffini was absent from the Council this morning? He took a taxi and told the driver to take him to the Council. Then he got absorbed in his *Osservatore Romano*. After a long time he looked out the window and saw cows grazing in a meadow. 'Where are you taking me?' he bellowed. 'Where you told me, Your Eminence. We are already halfway to Trent.' "

An old priest who had been listening, with what I took for disdain for too often repeated jokes, suddenly smiled and added his own: "I have a riddle for you. Cardinals Ottaviani and Ruffini and Archbishop Felici went out fishing in St. Peter's bark. A terrible hurricane started and swept all three of them overboard. Who do you think was saved?" That one had circulated too long; both bishops cried in unison: "St. Peter's bark!"

I shall always be grateful to Father Murphy for the opportunity to draw the celebrated Redemptorist moral-theologian Father Bernard Häring, expert at the Council and author of such profound works as *The Law of Christ* and *The Joannine Council*.

He was sitting in his neat, bare room in the Academia Alphonsiana, writing at a tiny table next to his iron bed, on which a stark, black crucifix was lying. His gothic head seemed to be copied from an altarpiece by Memling or Van der Weyden. Or had I seen it on the tombstone of a crusading knight? But if this was the head of a crusader, it was that of a crusader for·tolerance and decency. I heard Father Häring often as a speaker at the American Press Panel. What he had to say was always gentle and rational. The way in which he said it made one understand the meaning of the word charity.

And then destiny brought me Father Eugene Hoade, an Irish

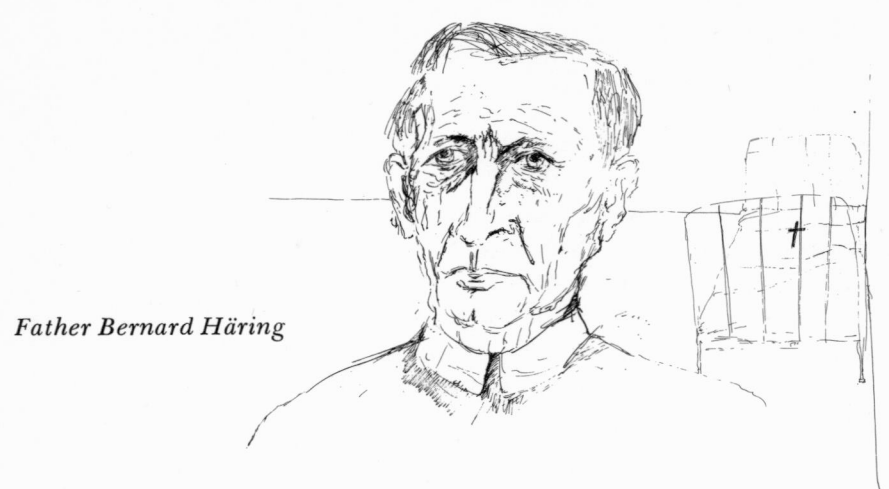

Father Bernard Häring

Franciscan in his fifties, with a craggy face, a melodious Irish voice, and a squat body in a stained brown habit. Blue eyes blazed in his ruddy face, a face belonging in the sixteenth century rather than the twentieth.

He was a confessor in St. John of the Lateran—"first shop on your left as you come in"—and was somehow in charge of the Oriental bishops during the Council. He spoke Arabic as well as he spoke English and had covered diplomatic missions all over the Near and Middle East.

"Whom can I get for you?" he asked bluntly.

"Well, Father, I am still very short on cardinals."

"Whom do you want to start with? I'll call him for you."

I thought the Franciscan was boasting. "Can you just call them?" I gasped.

"Look," Eugene Hoade said, "I have served this here Church for thirty years. I would be ashamed of myself if I couldn't get you a few cardinals."

"How about Agagianian?" I ventured.

"I'll call him up for you. And I'll take you to Cardinal Tappouni. And Paul-Pierre Méouchi, the Maronite Patriarch of Antioch, if you wish." We started with Cardinal Tappouni. The old dusty palace of Cardinal Tappouni lies behind the Pantheon, hidden by a wide door that looks as if it were the entrance to an old coach house. We crossed an unkempt, quiet courtyard. A fairly young man in clerical clothes with a short, Henry IV beard appeared and greeted Father Eugene like an old friend. They immediately burst into Arabic and seemed to forget all about me. Then later they obviously talked about me. For my benefit, Father Eugene translated a bit and I began to notice that he introduced me more or less as if I were his private juggler or acrobat—A quite amazing find: he draws portraits in ten minutes! Damn good, too. "Look!" he would cry triumphantly, "there you are, Your Eminence! What did I tell you!"

Somehow this did not disturb me too much. I fell in a little with my role of drawing-phenomenon, immediately started to draw, with a smile of "Ladies and gentlemen, you will now see the fastest drawing trick in the world! Nobody, but nobody, has ever broken my record. At the Olympic games in Tokyo, I outdrew the Chinese by 0.17 seconds! . . ."

It was a sort of protective mask Father Eugene had unwittingly invented *ad majoram Dei gloriam*, and I was grateful for it. Behind this mask I could quietly observe these faces of the Roman Church: spiritualized faces sometimes, or brutal faces, ambitious and resigned faces—few mediocre ones.

The old Cardinal Tappouni was waiting for us. He was still the only Oriental patriarch who is also a cardinal. He wore the scarlet hood of the patriarch. He was sitting on a low thronelike chair in his vast gilded drawing room, white thin hands in his scarlet lap. The face too was the transparent one of an ageless sage, of a legendary Assyrian king totally disenchanted and weary of this world of power and ambition. The suspicious, darting Levantine eyes of his assistant, Bishop Mansourati, had disturbed me at first, but the parchment and ivory of the fragile old patriarch made me forget the younger man. I left the Turkish coffee untouched, but had to accept a cigarette from His Eminence—"so I can smoke too," he urged very graciously.

Father Eugene had a special way with cardinals. Coming into the room he made a sketchy genuflexion and kissed the ring respectfully. Then he took the cardinal by the shoulder and smiled: "Well, and how have *you* been lately, Your Eminence?"

I had time to do three drawings of Cardinal Tappouni in that faded palace room, while my companions drank coffee and smoked and a steady stream of Arabic seemed to come from three sources at once.

Next day I had to call at Cardinal Agagianian's residence. Father

Cardinal Tappouni, Patriarch of Antioch

Eugene had waved his magic wand. Gregory Peter XV Cardinal Agagianian: Prefect of the Congregation of the Propagation of the Faith, nicknamed the Red Pope—because, some say, he is second only to the Pope in importance, or, others say, because of all the blood shed by Catholic missionaries. The prefect heads all the Church missions and governs hundreds of thousands of priests, nuns, and hundreds of millions of faithful all over the world. He had been the favorite *papabile* after the death of Pius XII in 1958; it was said that only his non-Italian birth prevented his election. I had an appointment with him at noon. The *portiere* at the Cardinal's palace looked inquiringly at the big black portfolio, then at my mock-ecclesiastical outfit, and asked: "Are you a Catholic or a Protestant priest, Father?" I explained that I was a *pittore,* a painter, and had an appointment with His Eminence at twelve.

In the bare, square waiting room I felt quite nervous. I'd better kiss his ring, I thought. After all, for kings you bow, or, if you are a woman, make a curtsey; for generals you salute. Moreover, I have no objections whatsoever to the idea of a hierarchy. A little old monsignor appeared. "I am Monsignor Giacomo," he explained, "and I am so terribly sorry, but His Eminence was detained at the Vatican. Would you mind very much seeing him at the Propaganda Fide on the Piazza di Spagna at five this afternoon?" Monsignor Giacomo was all smiles and apologies and charm; he ran out with me to the door, sending the young porter ahead to call a taxi. The general courtesy of Catholic Rome began to exercise a tremendous charm on me. It reminded me of another age, vaguely remembered from a long-lost Europe.

At five I was at the Propaganda Fide, perhaps the most tastefully appointed official building belonging to the Vatican. The hall is light and cheerful, contemporary in buff marble, with a genuine twentieth-century elevator. The waiting rooms are vast and tasteful. The Cardinal had not yet arrived.

In one waiting room, fifteen or sixteen bearded mission bishops were reading their breviaries. There was absolute silence. In the other waiting room ten African bishops sat huddled together around a table. They chattered in a French I remembered from Brazzaville and Douala. The nearest African, very round and ebony-black, spoke to me.

"You are not a bishop, are you?"

"No, Excellency, I am an artist. I have to draw His Eminence later. I take it you are an African? From Gabon, by any chance?"

"Yes, I am African," he said. "But I am from Congo-Leo. I am the Bishop of Kikwit."

"I know Kikwit," I announced. "I remember Kikwit and will always remember it. I once flew to Mosango in an antique Piper Cub of Air Brousse and near Kikwit we ran out of gas. I was grateful for Kikwit then, and for your little airstrip! Running out of gas in the jungle is unhealthy."

The Bishop was as happy as if he had met a brother Kikwittian. "Oh," he said, "I wish you could draw my portrait too!" "It is a bit dark here," I observed, "but since we both have to wait, why don't we look for a lighter place?" We started exploring the geography of the Propaganda Fide and landed in the men's room, where there was not only a bright electric bulb, but even a broken-down chair.

I settled His Excellency on the chair and started to draw furiously. With all the waiting prelates, the Cardinal would have his hands full for a while anyway. The bulb was shining too straight down on the Bishop's head, making his face into a homogeneous black blob, but he was talking so animatedly about his need for a million dollars to set up a seminary in Kikwit, and insisting that I must surely know plenty of rich Americans who would be more than happy to give it to him, that I didn't dare have him shift his improvised episcopal throne. Now and then a bearded bishop would enter, and look at us in astonishment while pulling up his purple robe. We had hardly returned to the waiting room when the elevator opened and Cardinal Agagianian breezed past, waving his hat exuberantly at the waiting bishops and the lone *pittore*.

Two minutes later, as a liveried servant led me to the Cardinal's office, I felt the silent, bearded bishops staring at my back.

The Cardinal was sitting behind his desk. He looked up and his smile was at the same time quite mild and terribly shrewd.

El Greco's Cardinal at the Metropolitan flashed through my mind, and also, "the Mikoyan of the Pope."

"What language do you speak?" he asked quickly, nervously.

"English, German, French, Dutch—whichever you prefer, Your Eminence."

He said in easy English, "How long do you need for your sketch?"

"Until you throw me out."

"Well, you have seen my waiting room," he said, lifting his eyes to heaven and spreading his hands like an overworked dentist.

Cardinal Agagianian

"Please do not let me disturb you—" I started my speech. But Agagianian was already signing letters, hurriedly, almost wildly.

I dived into my drawing. I liked this all-intelligent face. The thick, sensuous lower lip in the freshly trimmed pepper-and-salt goatee moved or trembled when he read. He worked in a fury.

Maybe ten minutes later, a footman knocked and whispered something about a *Principessa*. Gregory Peter XV softly hit his forehead with his palm and shook his head. He had forgotten the Princess completely.

"I have to interrupt you for five or six minutes—" he apologized.

"Oh, thank you, Your Eminence, I think I have all I need. I got on well with you."

"But you can come back," he said, as he got up and spread his hands at hip-height.

"No, Your Eminence, I really have all the notes I need."

He shrugged his shoulders. "It will only be a few minutes."

But I liked my drawing. It was precisely Agagianian as I saw him. So I smiled and kissed his ring the way it should be done. Not like a peasant on both knees and practically licking it, not like a *petit bourgeois,* all the way down to the floor, but the way Father Eugene did: a symbolic genuflexion, a symbolic kiss.

Yes, I liked my drawing. Months later Cardinal Cushing of Boston would see it and start arguing: *"That* isn't Agagianian. I know him. I gave him millions of bucks for his missions. That is *not* Agagianian."

I resented that. "Your Eminence," I observed icily, "Bishop Reilly liked this drawing and recognized Cardinal Agagianian immediately."

"Bishop Reilly is a very charitable man, a very charitable man! But that is *not* Agagianian!" Cushing shouted. He pronounced it "Aggy-johnny-ann."

"Then who is it?" I asked heatedly.

"That," bellowed the cardinal, "that"—pointing an accusing finger at my drawing—"that is Lenin!"

Cardinal Cushing, though he knew Agagianian so well, confessed later, with the great naturalness and humility of his noble soul that makes up royally for whatever may shock you, "Don't mind me. I don't know anything about art. I don't know good art from bad art!"

Cardinal Cushing

I was fast becoming a drawing automaton. Wherever I looked, my pen would start moving almost by itself. The six fountain pens in my shirt pocket had now leaked over my whole supply of white shirts. Rome had become my studio and a great elation was taking hold of me. After drawing a Brazilian cardinal in the Via Aurelia Nuova, I had to jump into a taxi in order to keep my appointment with a British archbishop on another of Rome's seven hills, or to draw at a theological conference where Cardinal Doepfner spoke at a briefing for international journalists, or to draw a bishops' luncheon. Something was happening all the time and mostly at the same time. There was no possibility of finding out any one day's schedule of meetings and events. The *Osservatore Romano* announced that Cardinal Suenens would speak at the Press Office, but of course omitted that at the same hour the German bishops had arranged a press conference at the German Center. How to choose? At the daily press conference of the Americans in a basement of the U.S.O. in the Via della Conciliazione journalists from twenty countries exchanged schedules at random.

"Tonight at five o'clock you can hear Father Weigel speak on Protestant Theology at the Gregorianum." "At five? But Cardinal Tisserant will be at the reception at the French Embassy!" "So how can I catch Cardinal Bea's speech at a quarter to six!"

I learned to draw at a gallop. The tension sometimes helped, sometimes paralyzed me. In taxis constantly caught in the eternal traffic jam that is Rome, I bit my nails while ruminating on the shape of the eyes or the form of the nose I had just drawn.

I would have loved to go to the French reception; I should have gone to draw Cardinal Bea at his lecture. When would there be another opportunity? But I already had an appointment with Bishop Philippe Naaba of Beirut in his study in the Palace of Santa Martha in the Vatican—a bull-like energetic man—and afterward had to draw the Melchite Patriarch of Antioch at the Hospital Salvator Mundi. The Patriarch Maximos IV Sayegh had been a force to be reckoned with at this Council from that first day, when he refused to walk behind the cardinals in the opening procession. To the patriarch, these cardinals were comparative "nouveaux riches": his patriarchate preceded the establishment of the cardinalate by centuries. Antioch was held to be St. Peter's first see before he came to Rome! Maximos was also the only Council Father who on principle refused to recognize Latin as the language of the Church: he always spoke French. In the course of the first and second sessions of the Council, this octogenarian with his spiritualized and aristocratic face made some

Father Weigel lectures

of the most important, incisive, and influential speeches. He was universally respected and not a little feared.

He was writing that first time not seeming to notice me, totally immersed in his work. Every now and then he looked up; fierce young eyes in an ancient face looked past me.

A little later, I sat opposite John Achkar, Greek-Catholic Metropolitan of Latakia in Syria, who lived in a tiny dilapidated hotel room, and who was the most loveable of all the prelates.

"Why do you want to draw me?" the rosy old man with his silken white beard asked. "I do not even look like a Levantine—well, *soit,*" he broke off. "But tell me"—he fingered his beautiful pectoral cross with a small ikon as its center—"do you want to draw the bishop or the man?"

"The man," I said, for this was really a human being after my heart.

"Fine," he said, "then I can take this thing off!" and he gently tossed his foot-high headdress on the bed.

It appeared he had for three years traveled in Africa to all mission posts below the Sahara "as a sort of rapporteur," as he called it. "Oh, I liked Africa, I loved the African people. But what a terrible cultural lag! It is so stupid to overlook or to gloss over it, to talk of equality where there is such divergence. One can love what is unlike oneself, *n'est-ce pas?* After all, I come from one of the oldest cultures. I feel Africa is totally unpredictable. . . . It is good that we get more and more African bishops, and at last a cardinal."

Then suddenly he spoke about Israel. "Of course, we are enemies. But many, many in my country admire in their hearts much that has been done there."

John Achkar, you were one of those in Rome, who, like Pope John, had left far behind them all animosity toward men, all hostile impulses, all hateful aggressiveness toward this creature that must die so soon anyway—one of those from whose every gesture flow blessing, understanding, wisdom, and compassion.

The next day, as I walked late into the daily American press conference in the basement of the U.S.O., the chairman, Father Edward Heston, was berating the correspondent of the unprincipled reactionary paper *Il Tempo,* which had just printed a libelous account of one of Father Gustav Weigel's lectures. Its correspondent, the very distinguished-looking Prince Ruspigliosi, stutteringly tried to defend himself, and that made Father Heston angrier and angrier.

The young priest at my side followed the progress of my drawing. "Oh," he whispered, "couldn't you come to my hotel tonight and draw me with Hans Küng? How much do you charge?"

"If I charged you, you wouldn't be able to raise the money, Father, but I'd like to draw Küng, so I'll be there."

I was there on time, but somehow I could not draw Küng as I wanted to. Maybe it was because I was compelled to listen to every word this wonder-boy of the Council had to say. This young Swiss theologian, who had succeeded Karl Adam at the University of Tübingen, had expressed thoughts in his book *The Council, Reform and Reunion* that had affected me deeply and shown me the Church in a new light:

The idea of the Holy Church, distinct from her often unholy members, mentally hypostatized into a sort of pure substance, is a dangerous abstraction. . . . Catholic reform, being renewal, lies midway between two extremes, revolution and restoration. . . . Think of the disastrous confusion of tradition with "traditional" (but perhaps extremely recent) customs, of orthodoxy with uniformism, of the discipline of the Church with legalism, of veneration for Mary with Marianism, of ecclesiastical institutions with institutionalism. . . . Reunion will then be neither a Protestant "return" nor a Catholic "capitulation," but a brotherly approach from both sides. . . . Most dogmatic definitions have been drawn up against heresies and are then neither more nor less than defensive barriers. . . . The scriptural concept of the Body of Christ, of which *all* Christians are members. . . . The layman does not belong to the Church in some secondary sense, but he *is* the Church.

I had not realized then how much the Curia hated Küng. He had been prudent enough to have his book preceded by two introductions, one by Cardinal Koenig, the other by the noble Achille Cardinal Liénart. Yet it was rumored that the Holy Office had indirectly tried to prevent Küng's writings from being sold in Rome, and had attempted to prevent an American translation. A few decades ago Hans Küng might have been excommunicated; a few centuries earlier he might have been found worthy of the stake.

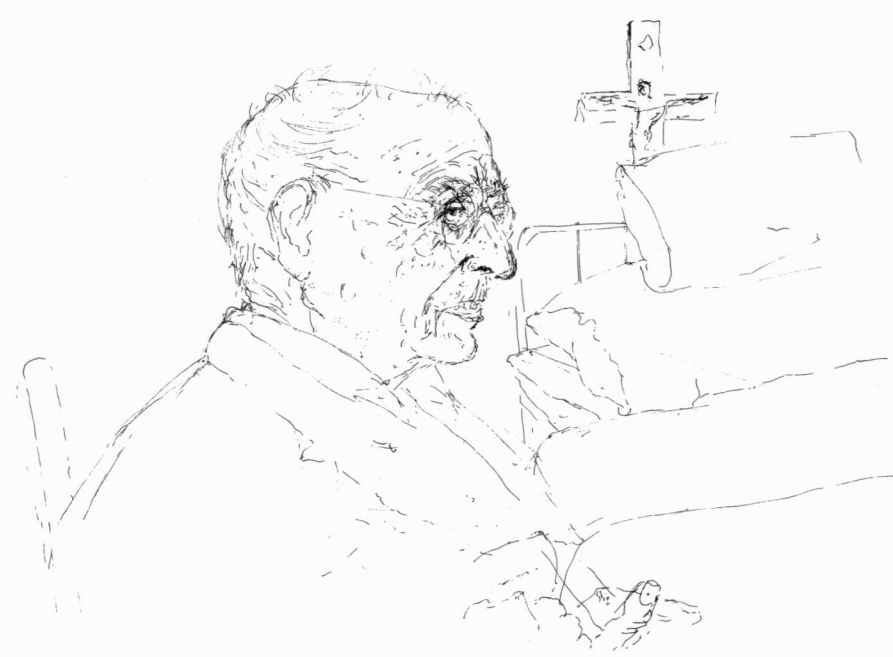

John Cardinal D'Alton, Primate of All Ireland

Now he was at the Council as an expert, and his lectures were heard by overflow audiences. Times were changing rapidly—and the Church with them! Küng the writer was one of my heroes; Küng the man I could not draw easily. Something—his ego, his ambition, perhaps— stood in the way. Or perhaps the profound awareness and sharp intellectuality of this mind had not yet found time to chisel the still boyish face. He reminded me too insistently that he was there—all Küng. The mysterious contact in which I become merely the hand that notes down was not established, and nothing can fake it; I am no camera; I become inhibited. While drawing Archbishop Descuffi, however, or Botéro Salazar, or Cardinal D'Alton, I could completely forget myself.

Yet I wonder if I would have felt much affinity with the ideas of John Cardinal D'Alton, Primate of All Ireland, who sat sick and old in his hospital room. Father Eugene took me to see him. The young and devoted secretary whispered into my ear: "Please don't make it long, and don't let him talk too much. He is so exhausted."

The Cardinal, who was nearly eighty, was sitting next to his bed, in an old faded ulster. He was shivering a little, and behind his glasses the light blue eyes, bleached by age, looked as if they too were made of glass. "I am too weak to travel now," he told Father Eugene, with whom he was reminiscing about people they had both known in Galway. "Maybe next week we'll go back to Ireland."

His voice was nearly inaudible, and this pianissimo Irish was touching and very beautiful. He recalled the death of one of his predecessors when he was still a young priest. "He was such a kind man, the old Cardinal," he whispered. I saw the old man's face develop itself on my paper quite magically as in a trance, and as quickly as an overexposed film in new developer. "The old Cardinal lay there dying and just before the end he said to us young priests: 'Boys,' he said, 'look behind the curtain in yonder corner. You will find a bottle there,' he said. 'I want to see you have a drink before I go.'"

A week or so later old Cardinal D'Alton himself had gone to his rest.

Another love at first sight was His Beatitude Stephanos I Sidarous, Coptic Patriarch of Alexandria. For it is love at first sight or it is a blank, and the drawing goes accordingly.

His was a young face, serious and strong. There were no pretensions. "Shall I put on my crown for you?" he asked humbly, fingering the bejeweled royal headgear.

"Oh, Your Beatitude, first I think I'd like you without a crown." In Ethiopia, I had been deeply moved during Coptic services, shaken by the fervor and beauty of the chant and by the mystery of the consecration, enacted behind the ikonostasis, a screen that hides the altar from the faithful.

Stephanos Sidarous was delighted with my drawing.

"Shall I send you a photostat of it, Your Beatitude?"

He seemed to ponder this. "No," he said at last, "bring it at the second session. I never know whether I get my mail in Alexandria. We are a bit suspect, we Copts, we are a kind of insecure minority in Egypt." He gave me a book on Egyptian Copts and wrote a dedication to me, *"qui aime notre Eglise Copte."*

I had only the vaguest notions about those Melchites, Copts, Maronites, and other Orientals and their ties to the Holy See, but found out that the so-called Uniat churches are fractions of the independent Eastern churches that seceded from the parent body to ac-

*Cardinal Patriarch
Stefanos Sidarous*

cept the supreme authority of the Pope, but that retained their own organization and liturgy. Their divisions are very complicated. Suffice it to say that there are four main groups among the Oriental Catholics: First comes the Byzantine rite, under the Patriarch of Antioch and of all the East. Maximos IV Sayegh, of the Melchites, and the Greek Exarchate, to which also the Ukrainian rite belongs. Then there are the Syrian churches, of which the Maronite Church is best known. They also have a Patriarch of Antioch, Paul-Pierre Méouchi. A third group is the Coptic Church, under the Patriarch of Alexandria, Stephanos Sidarous, and a fourth is the Armenian Church, which also has its Patriarch and Katholikos of Cilicia.

My next model was the householder of one of these Eastern mansions, the Maronite Patriarch Paul-Pierre Méouchi. When I got to his palace His Beatitude had not yet returned from the Vatican. A bearded old man with young keen eyes, the black Maronite hood pulled back over his head, was sitting in a dingy little room near the entrance of the palace. His fingers were cigarette-stained; he smoked constantly. His French was staccato and yet sing-song. A very young priest was joking with the old man as he served Turkish coffee. "He was only ordained yesterday," he said, pointing at the young priest, "and I am about ready to die." The keen eyes were having great fun. I pulled out my sketchbook and started to draw. "Let me put on my ring and my cross; I am the Father Superior here." The old man fumbled in a drawer.

The Patriarch came home, and the young priest guided me to a darkish salon through long rooms, all reddish and very oriental with low taborets and purple hangings and an aura of heavy perfume. It was moth-eaten and yet impressive; not exactly clean yet somehow well kept. The little inlaid tables, the red velvet curlicued settee, the chandeliers, the low gilt-and-velvet stools with dachshund legs—how strangely familiar it all looked! Did I remember it from a previous incarnation when I may well have visited Levantine drawing rooms? Or did it return to me from some book or film long forgotten? Were there really peacock feathers in a vase on the ornate mantelpiece? Were there bearded patriarchs or odalisques in the ornate frame? Were there vases of perfumed artificial roses on a green marble pedestal with gilded grooves like a Doric column?

Cardinal Patriarch Paul-Pierre Méouchi

The Patriarch came in. He was tall and powerful, around seventy, majestic in scarlet habit with red skullcap.

"*Voulez-vous que je me mette ici, sur le divan?*"

"*C'est parfait. Excellence.*"

"*Votre Béatitude,*" he corrected me kindly. Indeed, patriarchs are Beatitudes, cardinals Eminences, bishops Excellencies—"Pardon!"

I liked his face immediately. It was severe. Our conversation was accordingly most formal.

"*Vous aimez Rome?*"

"*J'adore Rome, Votre Béatitude.*"

"*Vous avez déjà dessiné beaucoup? Le Père Eugène me dit que vous avez fait un très beau dessin du Cardinal Tappouni.*"

"*Le Père Eugène est trop gentil, Votre Béatitude.*"

As time went by, his face became much less severe and tense. It had great mildness, I noticed while drawing the left eye.

"*Je connais très bien votre pays,*" he said suddenly.

"*Vous connaissez mon pays, Votre Béatitude? Vous voulez dire la Hollande ou l'Amérique?*"

"*Les Etats Unis, je veux dire. J'y ai habité quatorze ans comme prêtre.*"

"But then you must speak English?"

"Sure do," he said with jollity. "Like the best of them! I used to live in Brooklyn, see, and in California, too."

He spoke Brooklynese with the perfect academic accent. His face was radiant now.

"Did you ever get back?"

"Sure. Last year I went all over the place. Boy, has it changed! I went all over the West Coast, too. I was the first Catholic priest to be photographed with President Kennedy!"—he pronounced it "foist"—"I had dinner with Vice President Johnson and his wife."

"You must have had a wonderful trip after so many years, Your Beatitude. What did you like best?"

The Patriarch thought for some time. Then his eyes lit up till he was all a-twinkle. "Disneyland," he said.

Bishop Jan Klooster, in all his innocence, had prepared my integration into the Roman life around the Council in a masterly way. The Casa Unitas, the convent-hostel in the Via dell'Anima, proved to be as felicitous a choice of residence as possible. A room within the walls of the Vatican itself could hardly have offered me better contacts. When I entered the modest door in the Via dell'Anima with my suitcase and my portfolio and took the little elevator, I still expected the Casa to be a banal *pensione* in a restored apartment of the old building. I did not suspect that I would be staying in one of the most grandiose palaces of Rome, the Palazzo Doria Pamphilj, built by the august, princely family of Doria Pamphilj that gave popes to the Church and admirals, soldiers, and administrators to Italy for centuries. The Palazzo, built around the lofty baroque Church of Sant'Agnese, covers half the length of the Piazza Navona. One wing now houses the Brazilian Embassy, the other the Casa Unitas and the International Unitas Association, one of the first associations of Catholics interested in Christian ecumenism, anticipating the aims of the present Ecumenical Council.

The ideals motivating the Unitas Association found their first expression in the initiative of Luigi Cardinal Lavitrano, of Palermo, who in 1929 initiated a movement for union with the Eastern churches, and in 1941 started a center for the reunion of the churches. After the war, new dynamism was added by the work of an Italian priest who, returning from imprisonment in Siberia, vowed to devote the rest of his life to the unification of human beings, and especially to the reunification with the Holy See of the Russian Orthodox Christians. In 1945, an association for the promotion of Christian unity, comprising priests and laymen, was formed under the presidency of Father Charles Boyer, S.J., professor of philosophy at the Gregorianum (Gregorian University), who was much encouraged by Cardinal Tisserant and the present Pope Paul. With the support of Cardinal Pizzardo, the Association was approved in a warm letter signed by the then Monsignor Giovanni Battista Montini, as pro-Secretary of State under Pius XII.

Father Boyer, who was no doubt appointed in order to keep a watchful eye on the then not yet fashionable ecumenical enthusiasm of a group of young Catholics, was to see the seeds sown by his pioneers flower with a vitality beyond his wildest dreams—and perhaps even his wishes. For he is a conservative theologian, confidant of Cardinals Pizzardo and Ottaviani, who still use him to write triumphalist, flowery but reactionary articles in the *Osservatore Romano* at critical junctures.

The present connection of the Casa Unitas with the Unitas Association is just a coincidence. They are merely housed in the same building, and they cooperate. My hostesses, the Ladies of Bethany, founded it with the intention of "offering non-Catholic pilgrims to Rome hospitality and guidance." The word "pilgrim" is not taken too literally, except in the sense that, knowingly or unknowingly, we are all on our pilgrimage from cradle to grave, and quite apt at some moment or other to be confronted by Rome.

The Ladies of Bethany are an order of nuns. But they are rather special nuns. Neither their dress nor their house proclaims their vocation by external signs. They submit to nine years of preparation before they take perpetual vows in their religious order, which was founded in 1919 by a prophetic Dutch Jesuit, Jacques van Ginneken. Their aim is to be witnesses of Christ and His Church in the midst of a world of growing unspirituality, to be witness to their faith, especially among non-Catholics and those who have lost their connection with the Church. They try to put into practice Father van Ginneken's principle:

All those who work among non-Catholics have to have the greatest respect for the human soul and its eternal value, respect for its individual qualities and gifts, its personal destiny, its particular potentialities and drives. They have to be ever wary of the assumption that all are the same; then they will understand that they should not dare to exercise power over those who are entrusted to them and may only try to enter into dialogue with them. Conversion is not a struggle for power, but the opening of the eyes to divine truth.

As the Mother Superior, Sophia Huf, put it: "All that is humanly good is significant for our apostolate, and not just as a means to an end—an attitude that is rightly rejected as unfair—but because of its intrinsic value."

The hostel was run by five of these extraordinary nuns in high heels, fashionable dresses and hairdos, women who with their great culture and exquisite tact were ideal hostesses to Catholic theologians and Protestant observers alike. At their excellent lunches I met Cardinals Alfrink and Bea, sketched such prominent theologians as Karl Rahner, Gregory Baum, Ratzinger, Hamer, Thyssen, Schillebeeckx. Monsignor Willebrands, of the Secretariat for the Promotion of Christian Unity, was a frequent guest. Father Stefan Schmidt, Cardinal Bea's alter ego, was an intimate friend of the house.

Cardinal Frings of Cologne, who was a neighbor in the Via dell'-Anima, would occasionally come to tea.

On the floor below, in the solemn, heavily panelled library of the Dorias, conferences of theologians and liturgists were constantly going on. Protestant, Orthodox, and Catholic experts mingled informally, sipping sherry. The house I lived in was an ecumenical council in miniature, where the moves in the *aula* of St. Peter's were not only critically discussed but even anticipated. At breakfast I could hear the Protestant observers, living at the Casa Unitas, sharing their worries and hopes over developments with the monsignors. On Sunday mornings after Mass in the noble simplicity of the house chapel, our landlord, the Princess Orietta Doria and her husband, Commander Frank Pogson, often came for breakfast.

Hardly had I locked myself in my cheerful room to make notes when Miss Sophia, or Mary or Teresita, would knock on my door to announce an important conference at the Biblical Institute, to give me tickets for a concert that all the cardinals would attend, or particulars about an appointment they had made with a bishop I wanted to draw. Best of all, they encouraged me, for they were always eager to look at my drawings. In the beginning I was afraid they might be shocked, for my drawings were not always reverent. But I found that my nuns had a healthy eye for humbug, a fine discernment for hypocrisy. They astonished me constantly by the freedom they allowed to blow through their house, the criticisms they voiced, their total disregard of rigid formulations, their spiritual earnestness, and their optimistic confidence about the renewal they expected from the Council for the Church and even for the world.

One day at the end of November, when rain was pouring down over the red roofs, I was sitting in my room when Miss Huf stormed in triumphantly. She had succeeded in arranging a special audience for me with Pope John! At last I could see him from close by. There would be only a small group. I might be able to draw him, even talk to him. The invitation was officially confirmed the next day by a messenger from the Vatican. When our small group walked excitedly past the Bronze Door we were told that unfortunately the audience had suddenly been cancelled. The Holy Father was in bed—he was indisposed.

"A cold" . . . "a stomach upset" . . . "anemia" . . . "prostate trouble"—for the next few days all Rome was making diagnoses. The

. . . a conference in Casa Unitas

gentle Indonesian Archbishop of Bandung shook his fine Javanese head sadly while I was drawing him.

"In the Council they say he has cancer," he whispered. He offered me a cigarette, took one himself. "My heart is not too good," he smiled, "and my doctor doesn't want me to smoke, so don't tell him." He was a childlike man, this archbishop. "Do you realize," he said, "that I was still a Moslem when I was fourteen years old? I was converted then. Isn't it fantastic that I should have become an archbishop? When I return to Indonesia next month, President Sukarno will send his car to meet me at the airport. He sent it to take me there too! His newest car!" He lit another cigarette and looked so very humanly proud. Like a man who had started as a peddler with a pushcart and now was the greatest banana wholesaler in Cincinnati or Amsterdam. Then he spoke about Pope John again, the way they all spoke of him, with the utmost gentleness and humble homage: "For him all men are really equal," he said.

Archbishop Sugijapranata was met at the airport by Sukarno's car, I suppose. I sent him a photostat of the drawing. His secretary wrote me that he had suddenly died.

Rumors of the Pope's illness were now part of every conversation. They changed day after day. "What about the Council?" I asked Father Eugene. "It will continue next fall under a new pope," he said in his gruff, matter-of-fact way.

On Thursday, December 6, it was sunny and cold. I stood all alone on St. Peter's Square, in the section where you had to have a pass. I was going to meet Bishop Jan Klooster for coffee. Afterward, practically next door, the General of the Salvatorian Fathers would pose for me. I was looking forward to drawing Father Schweitzer, with his craggy German peasant's head, and to the kirsch from his *Schwarzwald Heimat*. He served it in a trick glass that still looked full when it wasn't, and laughed at my efforts to empty it until tears came to his eyes. "Ach," he gasped, shaking with laughter, "you don't know how many bishops have fallen for that!"

Normally the session ended around twelve fifteen; then the "purple waterfall" began to pour forth. This time, at a quarter to twelve, while I was sketching two *carabinieri*, the doors of St. Peter's opened and bishops started to stream out onto the Square. I recognized the leonine head of Cardinal Tisserant, the calm, noble profile of Cardinal Liénart, and the ravaged, eagle's face of Cardinal Gerlier.

. . . a cold? anemia? A stomach upset?

The Pope was going to give his blessing to the Council Fathers from his window. I started to draw at random all around me. Someone stepped on my toes and said something polite. It was Cardinal Wiszynski. All about me swarmed the twenty-five hundred bishops and cardinals. I was the only layman drowned in this sea of scarlet and purple. The window opened. Terribly far away he looked, our Pope John, waving at us. And then the strong voice sounded through the loudspeakers intoning the Angelus. There was a roar from the Square which must have reached the Pope. As always with him, heart had spoken to heart. As if to reassure us all, he said: "Slowly, slowly, I am coming up. Sickness, then convalescence. What a spectacle we see before us today. The Church grouped together in full representation. *Ecco* its bishops, see its priests, see its people—a whole family is present—the family of Christ—Father, Mother, and Beloved of us all." He did not speak to a crowd, he spoke to each of us individually.

[83]

I listened and glanced around me, glanced at all those faces looking up. There was no doubt in my mind: they all knew he was fatally ill. They were deeply moved, but I did not see tears. The whole Square was filled with that particular lost, gentle smile people have when they realize something very dear is about to go forever. The strong voice continued, started to sing and to pray, and to bestow its blessing. The twenty-five hundred men in purple and scarlet were on their knees now, joined the chant and bent their heads in silence.

Early on Saturday morning, the eighth of December, 1962 some sixty photographers and one man with a sketchbook stood shivering in front of the Portone di Bronzo. They were the heavy artillery of world photography. They looked a quiet, chronically disgruntled lot. They were gentlemen, not that rabble of locusts that, in Italy especially, seems to swarm around and over any actress, accident, or miracle. Not the fighting buzzards, descending in scores wherever the smell of blood is even faintly discernible. I had seen those once, unforgettably, at work at the Albert Schweitzer Hospital in Lambaréné, clambering over the beds of the sick and the dying to get

Cardinals Spellman and Tisserant

their shots. "Poor fellows," Schweitzer had said, "to have to earn a living in such a way."

These were the very cream of international press photography—*Life, Match, Look, Frankfurter Illustrierte*—They had lugged their tripods, fit for antiaircraft guns, their huge leather cases, through the milky morning mist. At eight-thirty Tenente Martelli, of the *gendarmeria Pontifica*, appeared. The shivering men came to life with smiles, jokes, and handshakes. Martelli knew them all and was his friendly self, the strict but humanitarian man of discipline. He too seemed to think: "What a way to make a living." Photographers' passes were checked perfunctorily; there was no real need. All these faces were known.

"I apologize for giving you a photographer's pass," Martelli had said to me. "We haven't anything special for anachronisms like you!"

"Anachronism!" I had thought, going down the Scala Regia, the enormous grand staircase leading to the Bronze Door, past the gendarmes in Napoleonic tricornered hats; the Swiss guard in their fifteenth-century *Landsknecht* garb, designed by Raphael or Michelangelo, striped yellow and blue like heraldic mobiles swinging around halberds and lances; the barefoot, tonsured Franciscans in their medieval brown habits; the cardinals with seven-foot trains; the canons of St. Peter's in moth-eaten ermine capes—anachronisms all. I felt quite at home among these, my fellow anachronisms, watched with such great expectancy by a world that felt itself so proudly, if insecurely, jet-aged.

Not that I really believe that the artist, whose response to life is to draw, is an anachronism. He is perennial. He started to draw bulls and bison thirty thousand years ago in the caves of Altamira and Lascaux and he is still going strong. He is still trying to catch the sacred totem, Life, not in order to copy it but in order to come to terms with it, to possess it, to cherish it. The reflex of the eye following and the hand simultaneously tracing is somehow a magic act, a particular way in which this fleeting life is captured, realized, and celebrated.

When Martelli gave the sign, the heavy artillery forgot its smiles and its dignity. It charged, dragging its weapons along. The battle for the best spots had started—actually, for the next-best spots. The men of Felici, the official Vatican photographers, would by now have occupied the very best spots, shabbily dressed in tails, their undertakers' faces set in oily piety, fingering their Rolleiflexes and Hasselblads so that even during the consecration they seemed to participate in a perverse reform of the liturgy, which required the shooting of flashbulbs and strobes.

I did not join the race. My fountain pens would have dropped out of my shirt pocket. Once inside St. Peter's, the photographers started to climb onto the platforms erected for them. If they did not break their necks dragging their cameras and cases up those perpendicular ladders, it was only because of some special protection the Basilica provides. The first ranks were already training their enormous telelenses on targets not yet present.

"Of course I can't draw from up there," I said to Tenente Martelli. He winked at me. "I know, just follow me."

He placed me in the first row of a tribune for dignitaries at the entrance to the sacristy. Below, nuns and monks were sitting in silent expectation. There was still an hour to go. Opposite me was the Altar of the Confession with Bernini's four enormous cedar columns. Thin, aristocratic Knights of the Order of Malta in their scarlet tunics, and fat bourgeois Knights of the Holy Sepulchre in white capes were filing into their places in front of the nuns. A Chamberlain of Sword and Cloak in his sixteenth-century Spanish court dress, his noble, hawk's features wreathed in turn-on, turn-off smiles for dignitaries, kept parading in front of me. He was at least seventy, but he enjoyed himself, his ruffles, his sword, and his slim legs.

In its wisdom, this church bestows playthings on its fools, gives medals to its vain, confers power on those who crave power incurably, provides magic for the naïve, reveals truth to its seekers, brings beatitude to its visionaries and enlightenment to its saints. The artist it delights by its poignancy, its holiness, its beauty, and its vanity. This Basilica of St. Peter is one of its many worthy symbols. The enormous baroque building with all that gold and all that sculpture is far from our northern conception of the holy, the *numinosum*. It breathes power and pomp. How much closer to our hearts are the sanctuaries of Chartres, Tournus, Vézelay, Amiens, Cologne, I had thought on earlier visits. Now I did not judge, for I was already drawing the baroque one superciliously finds amusing until one begins to draw. Then it becomes clear that one is drawing the very fullness of nature, of life. It is like drawing the infinite multitude of forms in a roadside hedge, a multitude the eye can scarcely encompass and unravel. And this was designed not by nature but by man! I was invaded by a feeling of enormous gratitude for being here. Each face seemed absolutely unique; the moment was one of unfathomable gravity.

The lights went on, the huge nave was filling up with more than two thousand bishops; the cardinals came filing in past me. Some I already knew. I knew Doepfner with his unbounded animal energy, and Suenens, the withdrawn intellectual. I had drawn Ciriaci, that eminent historian who looked like a soft pink Fernandel; Cardinal Spellman entered, trembling somewhat, a worried, small man. A dozen very old Curia cardinals—Moreno, Pizzardo, Copello, Giobbe—rolled in as if on very slow, uncertain roller skates hidden beneath their long scarlet skirts. Cardinal Ottaviani, to many the very devil of the Council: how sick he looked with his proud, small inquisitor's head superimposed on a pitiful goiter, a sick and poor old man, half blind, one eyelid sagging over a pale eyeball. Archbishop Dante, the Master of Ceremonies, with the face of a soldier, not a Brahmin at all but a Khsatrya, his eyebrows pulled up in chronic protocolar worry, frowned at my big sketchbook as he passed by.

I drew in fury of concentration, and suddenly, while I was turning

. . . as if on slow roller skates

it over, a paper covered with cardinals-on-casters slowly drifted down among the kneeling nuns. My heart stopped a moment. Two pale nuns turned their faces to heaven, from whence my drawing had definitely not descended. I made heartrending gestures, and the sheet rose up to me again on thin, white nun's hands.

The Mass had started, far away at the Altar of the Chair. From where I sat I could just see Cardinal Masella, who was the celebrant. The pontifical throne at the Confession Altar remained empty. The Mass proceeded; the Credo intoned by Cardinal Masella was joined by all those two thousand bishops of all nationalities, races, and rites. The kiss of peace was transmitted from cheek to cheek, and then Monsignor Willebrands, in his turn, brought it in the name of the Secretariat for the Promotion of Christian Unity to the non-Catholic observers. Something of overwhelming inwardness was happening in Bramante's extrovert basilica. Soon after the Pater Noster there was a stir on my left. Pope John had entered the Basilica, preceded by Noble Guards, their uniforms blotches of red and gold mingling with the scarlet patches of cardinals, an amorphous violet of archbishops, and the white and black and brown of monks. But my eye was focused on the one old man. He was not carried on his *sedia gestatoria,* but walked. The face I had seen smiling from so many photographs was serious but not tense. He looked about him, the head slightly bent; the eyes, darting sideways, swept over the nuns and for a second I looked straight into them. He walked rather fast with a firm step, but I was shocked by that peculiar bluish-pink pallor that early medical training had taught me to suspect. He climbed the steps to his throne with surprising agility, put on his glasses, then started his address in a clear and steady voice. His face did not show suffering; it was completely serene.

This portly man, this homely face, was now beloved all over the world by men of all faiths and no faith, a symbol of hope in human solidarity, of courage and of reason.

My hand refused to draw. I could only take him in, this man with the heavy body and the peasant face, who had only the one alternative to being a fat, jolly grandfather: to be sublime!

I heard him say: "The Council is an act of faith in God, of obedience to His laws and a sincere effort to correspond to the plan of redemption. . . . It has shown to all the world the holy liberty that the sons of God enjoy in the Church. . . . The first session was like a slow and solemn introduction to the great work of the Council. . . . It was necessary for brothers, gathered from afar around a common hearth, to make each other's close acquaintance."

Peering over his glasses, he exhorted the bishops to do their homework during the nine months before the second session, and urged them to bring the Council to a speedy close in order to satisfy the thirst of the peoples who were looking to it for concrete results. Then he once more walked past me with his strong step and disappeared through the side door from which he had entered.

Walking out of St. Peter's into the cold sunshine, I was just in time to see the old Pope once more at his window, blessing the densely packed crowd kneeling in St. Peter's Square, heard once more the warm, strong voice over the loudspeakers.

Then the window closed. Bishops and cardinals sauntered away in groups through the ecstatic crowd. A people it was, not a mob. A people hungry for spiritual sustenance in a baffling world had come and they had been nourished.

Superstition? Who dares make the accusation of superstition in our time, a time cursed with unparalleled paroxysms of superstition, the time of the *Sieg Heils,* the ritualistic burning of books and six million witches, the time that believes in the dropping of atom bombs to create peace, that believes in security guaranteed by ever greater engines of mass murder?

Could we be anything but baffled, we who were born under gas lamps and have lived to see the satellites launched, who have lived through world wars that made the shooting of hostages, the bombing of civilian populations acceptable practices, who have witnessed the invention of a new sin against the Holy Spirit, that sin against our mother the Earth called atomic testing, in which we, mere products of the earth's crust, violate it irreversibly and do incalculable villainy to millions of fellow creatures?

We who are superstitious enough to calculate casually the number who will survive mutual attempts at total annihilation, are we the ones to scoff at a church which, to say the least, provides one way of transmitting eternal verities and which is attempting to make them once more palpable to contemporary man? Under Pope John the Church had made a start in this heroic effort. It made the first gesture of reconciliation when it replaced such terms as "infidels," "apostates," "heretics," with the term "separated brethren." It has purged its liturgy of anti-Jewish formulations. It has asked forgiveness for sins it no doubt committed in the past, and which it now deplores as culturally determined betrayals of its mission.

It may be true that this was the logical conclusion of a process that started under Leo XIII, was frustrated by his successors Benedict XII and Pius XI, and that had motivated Pius XII, be it in carefully ambiguous rhetoric. Yet it was John XXIII who dared to recognize that the language of authoritarian religion is a dead language, that the juridical language of the official theologians by now can be decoded only by theologians. Without the sanctions of force, the impotent language of threat and condemnation has become as repellent as it is ineffective. Man is still willing to accept spiritual guidance and authority. But it is the authority of the beacon and the compass that he consults freely, not that imposed by the nursemaid or animal trainer. The great danger is no longer heresy or open schism, only because there is the so much greater danger of utter indifference or silent schism.

Man must have learned by bitter experience how the language of the Church had been tainted by centuries of abuse, heaped on those who dared to differ and had become associated in the modern mind with condemnation and excommunication, power and profits, pyres and pogroms.

There is a humanitarian language that modern man desperately craves. Pope John spoke this language of contact, reconciliation, love, and respect for each human person quite naturally, and so became the natural pontifex, or bridge builder. His bridge was built out of "dialogue," not only with Protestants but with Buddhists and Jews and atheists as well. Its stanchions were the Gospels, whose revolutionary message calls all establishments into question.

He was well on his way to neutralizing those "prophets of doom" who have stubbornly disregarded the social, scientific, technical, and psychological evolution of the last three centuries. In John, the Church demonstrated a clear consciousness of its own ethos. It became servant rather than tyrant, dispenser of grace, wisdom, and tenderness rather than of condemnation. Pope John accepted the fact that holiness and enlightenment cannot be dictated, and he embraced the saints and sinners of the world and of his own church as fellow seekers on the Way.

And so this fatally ill octogenarian restored man's belief in goodness

... a deathly ill octogenarian

and made the idea of God once more plausible to millions outside the Church and the Churches.

In fifty months of papacy he had abolished the fifteen-hundred-year-old delusion that the Spirit could triumph through deals with temporal power. In the security of his faith in God and man he had conquered the anxiety neurosis that had characterized the relations between the Church—a resentful, perpetually irritated, and aggressive dowager—and the outer world ever since the Reformation.

The Joannine Church had insisted on universality and love, on a dialogue between peoples and religions, on the unity of Christian churches and indeed of all those who, realizing the insufficiency of merely political, nationalistic, social, and material preoccupations, recognized the primacy of man's spiritual values—his need for participation in transcendence in terms of our time.

The Joannine Church had once more proclaimed the cosmic radiance of the Christ in Glory and had made Rome once more into what Teilhard de Chardin has termed the "Christological pole of the earth."

The first session was over.

[91]

Interlude

THE NEXT morning, December 9, as an ecclesiastical bonus, there would be a canonization. At eight-thirty there was the scramble of the photographers again at the Bronze Door. Tenente Martelli gave me a sign. As the photographers were climbing to their platforms, I followed him behind Bernini's throne of St. Peter's. Now I was really backstage. It was full of theatrical props, chandeliers, thrones, tables, chairs, candlesticks, sculpture, rugs. Precisely behind the throne was a row of urinals. One was occupied by a knight in Spanish court dress. Emerging on the other side, I found myself on a tribune for diplomats and other high dignitaries, immediately behind the seats for the cardinals.

"How about this?" Martelli asked with a smile. On my left, a haughty lady in black lace rearranged her mantilla. On my right, men in high gold collars, their swords and tassels at their sides, were conversing in whispered French. One of them, in a black cape with purple collar draped over his shoulders, was dark-skinned with those rare, noble features one sees only in Ethiopia. Just across the nave the Cardinal-Chamberlain, Masella, was taking his seat, then Pizzardo, Tisserant, and Fossato, of Turin. Behind me, priests and nuns filled the back benches. To my left, near the Altar of the Confession, processions with liturgical banners carried by pilgrims from the birthplaces of the three people who were to be canonized filled the nave.

When the Pope entered, seated on his *sedia gestatoria,* I felt a shock. He looked ten years older than he did yesterday. The short trip on the wobbly oriental contraption obviously made him feel more ill. There was the sharp, strange noise of applause in the sanctuary, during the singing of *Tu es Petrus*. The old man sat on his throne, received the obeisance of four cardinals, and looked in front of him with unseeing eyes. I saw Cardinal Ottaviani approach him. He obviously inquired politely: "How are you feeling today, Your Holiness?" The old man made a quick gesture with the flat of his hand against his stomach and very faintly shook his head, pulling his mouth down a little. Then he looked before him into empty space.

On his left, the Master of Ceremonies, Monsignor Dante, was making his precise military gestures of command, his eyebrows raised, the thin mouth prim, like that of the headmistress of a girls' boarding school. The heavy vestments were now put on the old Pope, weighing him down, and the miter was placed on his head. When he was seated again, a terrible sadness descended over John's face and an expression of gnawing pain. Arcadio Cardinal Larraona, prefect of the Congregation of Rites, now advanced to the throne and requested, "instanter, instantius, instantissime," the proclamation of the three new saints. Monsignor Amleto Tondini, Secretary of the Briefs to Princes, replied to him. Then the old Pope, nearly smothered beneath his vestments, lifted himself and began to sing the *Veni, Creator Spiritus*. His voice was strong and as he invited the Holy Spirit his face became transfigured. There was no more trace of fatigue or pain. Then he pronounced the formula of canonization of the three new saints and ordered them inscribed on the list of the elect entitled to the homage of the altars.

There was an enormous applause, and the Pope intoned the *Te Deum*, taken over by the choirs and the congregation. Pope John sat down again and the expression of lassitude and illness returned. I had time to draw him now. The lady in the mantilla tried to follow my lines. "Excusez-moi, Madame," I hissed, shielding my drawing with my left hand, and with such venom apparently that she turned away brusquely. Her mantilla slapped my face.

At this moment a procession advanced from the direction of St. Peter's main entrance as if emerging from the very distant past, from the very beginning of Western civilization; preceded by mace bearers in black-and-purple medieval garb, by knights in full armor,

. . . an expression of lassitude and illness

by monks and priests in choir vestments, the gifts to the Pope that accompany each canonization were carried to him. They are symbolical gifts: candles, gilded and silvered loaves, antique casks of pure gold filled with wine and water and cages with live doves and small singing birds.

As the doves were brought near and shown to him, I saw him smile and gesture. He looked like a boy now, fascinated by these birds, transported. Was he back in Sotto del Monte, on the farm where he was born? The tenderness and happiness remained on his face as he gave his benediction; then the miter was removed from his head.

Lifted once more on the *sedia,* again he looked deathly ill, like a quenched fire. But the applause aroused him from his suffering, and, just as he was opposite me, I saw him look around and such a smile appeared on the old face as I had never seen before. Pope John's smile was ecstatic. It was as if he realized all at once that he was among his friends, that each of these thousands of people saw him as he really was, and accepted and loved him. The smile remained and the eyes overflowed with vitality and joy. Playfully he threw a hand-kiss to some old friend on his right who must have caught his eye. It had not yet been enough for him. He still had to appear at his window and bless the crowds on the Square. He was clearly aware that he had very little time left. He didn't even listen to his doctors with their bedside lies and hypocritical counsels to rest and take it easy. How could a man like John have failed to see through these old professional tricks for the weak in spirit! I have known lesser men who politely gave their doctors the satisfaction of their well-played, well-meaning deceit. John had decided that his death was near and that he would spend himself in the cause he was identified with. He would spend his body and his spirit until the very last gasp.

Before leaving to board a plane for New York, I sat down in my room in the Casa Unitas. I started to look through my drawings for the first time, since while drawing, there is no time and no desire. There were a few hundred. Out of my window I looked at the dusk over old Rome. The sky was a coldish pink and gray. A drizzle fell again, fine as a haze. In the distance beyond the dome of St. Peter's the pylons of Radio Vaticano with their blinking little red lights were broadcasting the canonization to the world. In a room below me on the Via Santa Maria dell'Anima, on an old-fashioned oak bed under a bare bulb, a man and a woman were making love.

I decided that on this last evening in Rome I would write down what I had learned since the day when I had felt impelled to fly to Rome.

Pope John, then, had announced to his politely listening but flabbergasted cardinals on January 25, 1959, that he intended to call an Ecumenical Council. This in itself was a first demonstration of freedom by a man who was not only conditioned by his own eighty years of training in obedience, but who was also the product of some fifteen hundred years of conditioning. The idea itself was revolutionary. It was generally assumed that after the First Vatican Council—which broke up in 1870 when interrupted by the Italian civil war—established the dogma of the primacy of the pope and his

. . . politely listening but flabbergasted cardinals

infallibility in matters of faith and morals, the period of Ecumenical Councils was over. At that time, only optimistic clairvoyants like Cardinal Newman could be confident that one day a new pope would come who would call a new Council and "once more bring the boat in its proper course."

This new pope had arrived in John XXIII, that "interim pope" who would be so easy to handle! There was going to be a Council, and in the very act of calling it, John gave his own reinterpretation of the dogma of infallibility without in the least weakening it.

For three and a half years 841 cardinals, bishops, monks, and theologians prepared for this Council under the Pope's direction; 25,712 questionnaires went out; 2,150 replies to them were received from the prelates of the Church. Nearly 9,000 suggestions for improvements and reforms were contained in these replies, embodying all manner of self-criticism. The preparatory commissions accordingly composed some seventy schemata, or draft decrees.

During the first session of Vatican II, which lasted two months, five of these seventy schemata were discussed in Latin, which up to then had been regarded as the traditional, official language of the Church. It was learned that there were grave objections to Latin as a language for discussion: theoretically, as was made clear by the Eastern churches; practically, because of confessions of incompetence in the language by some of even the most important Council Fathers.

The schemata discussed were those on the Liturgy, on the Sources of Revelation, on Mass Communications, on Christian Unity, and on the Church. Thirty-five ballots were taken; objectively speaking, the results were scanty: only the Introduction and the first chapter of the schemata on the Liturgy were adopted. But contact had been made and conflict had been rife. It became immediately obvious that the Roman Curia cardinals who headed the preparatory commissions—theoretically nothing but the "working cabinet" of the Pope—had been disinclined to follow either the spirit of Pope John or the general climate of opinion among the bishops. The results looked like sabotage. Had the dominant spirit in the Curia succeeded, the Church would have become even more isolated in a self-imposed ghetto than before. But the freedom accorded by John to this "Open Council" of bishops prevented this. The first defeat of the Curia, in the person of Cardinal Ottaviani, Secretary of the Holy Office— which was called the Inquisition from the time of the Council of Trent until 1907 and which had succeeded in maintaining a stranglehold on the episcopate, the priesthood, the laity, and perhaps on the papacy, for four hundred years—came soon, on October 13, 1962. Archbishop Pericle Felici, spokesman for the Curia and Secretary General of the Council, announced one hundred sixty candidates for the ten working commissions. These were immediately rejected by the majority of the Council Fathers.

The alignments now became clear. The "progressives" (as the anti-Curia group was soon called) were the bishops from those countries where the Church had constantly to deal with non-Catholic populations, whether Protestant or secularized. They were, mainly: the French, under Cardinals Liénart, Feltin, Gerlier; the Germans under Jaeger of Paderborn, Doepfner, Frings; the Austrians under

Cardinal Koenig; the Belgians under Cardinal Suenens; the Dutch under Cardinal Alfrink; some Spaniards and most of the bishops from Africa and Asia. In other words, the "progressives" were all those who could no longer close their eyes to the painful reality that, notwithstanding church attendance records, the Church was in a state of crisis and that its relevancy to the modern world was in the balance; all those who had learned that in its conventional present form the Church had not brought, and cannot bring, nourishment to a contemporary society in which scientific, technological, and social developments occupy the center of human consciousness. The Church is in great danger of becoming an anachronism to contemporary man, a "pacifier whose flavor is almost gone." There is no time to lose, I heard Cardinal Suenens say, especially in view of the population explosion we are witnessing; a concrete program of reform is needed, not only by recognizing the social forces at work but also by a deepened realization of Christianity's essential message about the nature of man, his reality and his destiny, dropping ballast and unessentials overboard. The defeat of the forces of which Cardinal Ottaviani made himself the symbol had to be seen in this light.

Indeed, on October 30, Cardinal Ottaviani, after a speech exceeding the officially set time limit, accused the Fathers of starting a revolution, and in protest against his being held to the time limit stalked out not to return until a fortnight later.

The third defeat of the congealed orthodox group followed just a week later, when the schema on the Sources of Revelation was effectively voted down notwithstanding attempts by the Curia to confuse the voters. Pope John intervened, not as an infallible dictator, but as the interpreter of the obvious consensus of the Council.

A turning point was reached, not only in the proceedings of the Council, but perhaps in the destiny of the Church and even of mankind. The Counter-Reformation ended on November 21, 1962, some observers have said, perhaps overoptimistically. A development toward diversity in unity became possible. Cardinal Bea, the wise progressive and humanistic biblical scholar, head of the Secretariat for the Promotion of Christian Unity (created by the Pope and totally independent of the established Congregations), was directed to cooperate with Cardinal Ottaviani in the preparation of a revised schema for the second session of the Council, ending, at least sym-

Cardinals Ottaviani, Léger and Bea

bolically, the power monopoly of the Holy Office. The choice between the extinction of the Church or of its mothball preservation as a dusty museum piece and a new surging life had been made, recognizing the unity of the world in its plurality. With it came the realization that for the Church too close involvement in the secular, political machinery is dangerous and ineffective in the contemporary world. Bishops from underdeveloped areas insisted that reliance on wealth and pomp had to be dropped, together with reactionary social and political attitudes still tainted with colonialism, and that the Church must identify with the poor and downtrodden. The era of triumphalist clerical imperialism of *Romanità* would have to be declared closed.

The really important task of the Council was to overcome the indifference, if not hostility, of the great masses, the building of bridges to the other Christians, the beginning of a dialogue with the great non-Christian world religions.

It seemed, then, at the end of the first session, as though the Church was ready to emerge from its isolation, ready once more to take its place amongst the living forces that shape world civilizations. Pope John's initiative had encouraged new aspirations.

These aspirations were: the possibility of increasing rapprochement with non-Catholic Christians; a greater political self-determination for Catholics in the West; a greater freedom and decentralization in the organization of the Church; a demonstration of the Church's spiritual renewal by showing true charity in its relationship to all peoples, regardless of faith and race.

Were we on the eve of a true renascence of the Church? Had Pope John, by humanizing his own office, succeeded in humanizing the Church, and even the world? He had shown himself not much more horrified by the atheistic materialism outside the Church than by the obscurantism and fanaticism within it as implements of the continuing martyrdom of man.

If he survived, a real renascence was bound to take place. If he must die, the "slow and solemn introduction to the great work of the Council" would not come to naught.

My response to Pope John's call had been to grab my sketchbook and to draw his Council. But the artist is a human being, and as a human being I could not fail to react totally to this great human and divine drama. I could not react as a theologian or a liturgist, but only as one whose eyes were involved—an observer in the most direct sense of the word—and whose spirit and heart, I hoped, were open.

I returned to my studio in Greenwich Village, but found myself still drawing, painting Council. My drawings were being published here and there, a large body of them was sold, requests for exhibitions were received from various places. One of these exhibitions took place in Boston at the time of Cardinal Bea's lectures at Boston University and Harvard. Pope John's closest collaborator spoke on religious liberty, not always a favorite subject with cardinals. Through the kindness of Cardinal Cushing I was able to present Augustin Bea, S.J., with an album of reproductions of my drawings on behalf of their owners, the St. Louis Priory. In the reception room of

Cardinal Cushing's "big barn," as he called his palatial residence, the big Irishman in scarlet moiré stood hovering over his frail colleague, pointing at the drawings. "That's you, Your Eminence!" he rasped, and "Look, there's your big pal Ottaviani!" "Ach, ist der köstlich!"—Cardinal Bea smiled his smile of an ancient Chinese sage.—"Oh, and that is the way you see *den Heiligen Vater!*"

A few days later I heard Cardinal Bea again in New York where he shared the rostrum in a colloquium with Protestant, Catholic, and Jewish theologians. U Thant represented the Buddhists, Zafrullah Khan, the Moslems. Again the Cardinal spoke passionately about religious liberty. When later, in Rome, I asked whose contribution he had liked best he answered immediately: U Thant's.

A few weeks later, on April 12, 1963, Pope John presented the world with the encyclical *Pacem in Terris*. Its very title again stirred the hearts of men. Sitting in my studio I read it until deep in the night. Pope John's testament to the world was written in a nonclerical language I felt I could understand, not in that traditional hyperbolic oratory that, hovering between earth and heaven, mystifies and fatigues.

Pacem in Terris squarely placed the Church in the world as its very conscience, as a mirror of the Gospel. It was the revolutionary charter of a new human order. Brushing aside the legalistic incrustations of centuries, it based this new human order on the realities of the human predicament in contemporary, pluralistic society, and on the dignity of human beings and their infinite potentialities. In it the Church, through its pope, suddenly becomes the champion of religious liberty, minority rights, constitutional government, and of a world community through international organization. It becomes once more plausible and relevant, as it limits its condemnations to injustice, cruelty, stupidity, and the abuse of atomic energy.

Pope John had written it in a race against death, hoping against hope that he might still integrate his prophetic insight into the body of doctrine of the Church, make its message clearly visible to contemporary eyes, make its members citizens of the world, placing the old Church suddenly in the advance guard of human evolution.

Sistine Chapel during the Conclave

Funeral and Conclave

Tʜᴀᴛ ɴɪɢʜᴛ after reading the encyclical I got up and had to draw John XXIII. I could not find my pen quickly enough, so I drew with the pipette of my ink bottle in a sort of trance that lasted a few minutes. By now everyone knew that Pope John was deathly ill. But that night I saw him in my mind's eye as the optimistic, forward-looking, ever-young mind he was, with the Holy Spirit at his side.

When the drawing was later reproduced on the cover of *America,* a letter to the editor protested: ". . . the Pope looks like an irate truck driver, the Holy Ghost like a plucked chicken. . . ."

It was not the only time the Holy Ghost had gone unrecognized.

For what John had to offer was the Holy Spirit who unites. He gave new meaning to the hackneyed formula, "Christian love." Immediately an unholy alliance of reactionary politicians, experts, diplomats, Vatican financiers, right-wing demagogues orchestrated a vicious campaign to discredit this novel encyclical that calls mundane matters like nuclear disarmament by name, asserts the right of man to his own religious and political convictions, stretches out its hands to unbelievers and even to communists, separating error from the human beings who err.

On June first, as Pope John lay dying, the same magnet that had drawn me to Rome in October began to pull again. I could not stand it in New York as I followed the excruciating radio bulletins hour after hour. Could I see him once more? I made a plane reservation.

But what could I do in Rome? This time there would be no press conferences, no bishops to draw. The cardinals would have other worries. The Conclave that would follow the now certain death of John XXIII would not exactly welcome an artist to do some sketches. It seemed an even crazier undertaking than the last one, this flight to Rome. But I wanted to see him once more. I was pulled as if my own father lay dying. At the same time, I felt I would be wasting my time and my money.

In my desperation, I thought that Cardinal Cushing, whom I had now met several times, might give me some technical advice. I phoned him in Boston.

"Of course you would be wasting your time," the gravel voice came over the wire. "You'll be standing in the Square with a million people. You asked me—let me tell you! You're crazy if you go; you're nuts."

The blunt Cardinal was right, obviously; I would stay home.

On June 3, 1963 at 3:49 P.M. the news came over the radio that John XXIII had ended his too long agony.

Only then I looked through that day's mail. It contained a letter from the Vicar-General of New York. I read:

It has pleased the Holy Father in appreciation of your drawings of the Ecumenical Council to confer upon you the Medal of His Pontificate. If you will call me I shall be pleased to . . .

This was too much for me. A few hours later I boarded the night plane to Rome.

It was near noon when I arrived, on an infernally hot June morning. The airport bus crept through dense traffic and leaden sunshine.

I left my luggage at the terminal and drove as close to St. Peter's Square as the taxi could get.

An endless stream of people had preceded me. The queue stretched for a mile down to the Tiber and it moved me along with it, half-asleep after the night-flight. In the middle of the Piazza, our line was split, and six abreast we were slowly pushed around the Obelisk. The crowd carried me up the slope, up the steps of the Basilica, and into the main entrance of St. Peter's. In semiconsciousness I read the sign forbidding photographs in St. Peter's, and saw the papal gendarmes. I got a nod of recognition from one; it woke me to the realization of where I was. My sketchbook went unnoticed. Then, at the catafalque I stepped back out of line and stood leaning against one of the grandstands for the Council Fathers, still in place.

He was lying on a high platform between Bernini's columns, flanked by Noble Guards and priests. His face had not changed, except that it was the color of bluish clay. The hands were stiffly folded. He was so high up that the stream of people did not obstruct my view. I stayed there for hours, pressed against the red material of the grandstand. The guards and the priests kept as immobile as the dead man. Gendarmes gently urged the line of people to move on. Pressed with me against the tribune were a dozen old peasant women. Were they allowed there perhaps because they had come from the Pope's village? I tried to draw, but it was difficult. In the half-dark I concentrated on his face. Then again on the mourners: old priests and people from Trastevere, mixed with elegant high bourgeoisie, peasants with flowers in their hands, and parents carrying babies and pointing at the dead Pope. A sunburnt peasant carried a heavy, man-sized wooden cross. It was so moving because there were no histrionics, no curiosity, no eagerness; it was a departure, a leavetaking. Our father had died.

The man I was drawing had been to me the fulfillment of the entire potentiality of man, the greatest man of my century. Toward the end he must have been completely enlightened. I saw this great Christian as a bodhisattva: one who, perceiving the highest Reality, does not withdraw into his beatitude but descends into the marketplace to bestow blessings and liberation on his fellowmen. Liberation from the futility of false aims, the frivolity of desires, the vanity of greed, the triviality of anger. Expressed in Christian terms, John was a man entirely filled by the Holy Spirit, the Comforter. Incapable of sham or pomposity, contemptuous of his own comfort and even his own life, he overflowed with compassion for others. All alone he dissolved the age-old, self-perpetuating image of the Church as the merciless plotter and revenger, a bitter, hard-bitten phalanx fighting its rear-guard battle in enemy territory.

In mankind's most desperate, lethal hour, John assured it that it was not doomed but called to essential oneness, *"that they be one."* And he calmly, smilingly, stopped the wheel that inexorably turns from antipathy to hatred, from hatred to violence, from violence to murder, and from murder to collective suicide.

His *Veni, Creator Spiritus* was an invitation that could not be declined. The Holy Spirit descended and made John speak words of compassion and reason to conquer the inertia of our non-spirit. In his last gigantic effort, his encyclical *Pacem in Terris,* he not only brought the Church up to date but also placed it in the vanguard of human evolution. Now millions of non-Catholics wept for him. He made Catholics forget how diabolical those unbelievers are, and, after four hundred years, memories of auto-da-fé and the Inquisition might at last be banished to where they belong: the history books.

The cynics are now reproaching you, Pope John, that you were naïve as a politician: may there be more of your politics of transcendence after all sophisticated *Realpolitik* has brought man to the brink of annihilation. May there be more of your statesmanship of the "new Pentecost," based on the knowledge that the frightened and starved human heart cannot but rapturously respond to love, respect, and compassion!

The doctors said that your dying took so long because your heart was so very strong. It still is beating. Death cannot stop it. . . .

At last I left my spot and was carried out of the Basilica by the crowd. The line still extended to the horizon. And as I stood on the side and drew the crowd again, while dusk was falling, I was to see him once more: so as not to disappoint those who had been too late to be admitted, Pope John's body was carried out once more to the steps of St. Peter's and shown to those who had loved him and to whom he had brought new hope.

Would he not have wished it precisely so?

When I woke up late next morning in Casa Unitas and saw my sketches of the previous day, I could not imagine how they had happened. I could not even believe I was back in Rome in that same room in which I had slept less than half a year ago. Pope John was buried. I was here to draw the funeral ceremonies, the Conclave, and the Coronation.

"Of course," said Tenente Martelli that next afternoon, as I sat opposite him in his dingy back room of the *gendarmería,* "I'd like to help you, but you know it is such a confused situation before the Conclave. I wonder if you shouldn't just write a formal request to the Cardinal-Chamberlain Masella. He is in charge of everything during the *sede vacante*." He dictated a flowery letter and I signed it. In it I asked for permission to draw in St. Peter's during the requiem masses, and in the rooms of the Conclave before its start. I went to see Father Eugene, the man who had the mysterious pass-key to all doors during the Council. He was just leaving for Ireland on holiday. Brother Welsh was leaving too; there would be no audiences until there was a new pope and so he was not needed in Rome. "You'll have a tough time this trip," Father Eugene had said. "But why don't you draw some bigwigs instead of biting your nails, and maybe one of them can help you. As an American, you should certainly draw Archbishop O'Connor. Go see Father Cunningham at Santa Susanna, he knows the Archbishop well and will call him for you."

Father Cunningham, the pastor of the American Church of Santa Susanna—a gray-haired, thin man with a face that looked ascetic from one angle, *gemütlich* from another—*did* call, and next morning I drove up to the North American Pontifical College, of which the Most Reverend Martin John O'Connor from Scranton, Pennsylvania, is not only the rector but also to a great extent the creator. When Monsignor O'Connor became rector of the college in 1946 it was housed in an ancient building in old Rome. It was he who built the magnificent College on Gianicolo Hill. He was named Titular Archbishop of Laodicea in 1959, and among his many high functions are those of Assistant at the Pontifical Throne, Consultor of the Sacred Congregation of the Propaganda of the Faith, member of the Central Preparatory Commission for the Ecumenical Council, and vice president of one of its conciliar commissions. He also heads the Press Committee of the Council. Ex officio, he is certainly the most important American cleric in Rome. He resigned as rector in 1964.

I found a huge man of sixty-three with a heavy florid face and very pale blue eyes that surprised you every now and then by a quick piercing glance. The very soft voice, I felt at once, concealed tremendous reserves of energy. Apart from a nearly imperceptible tremor of the hands, the Archbishop seemed to control each one of his movements with complete self-discipline. Yet nothing about him was stiff; the powerful body's movements were supple and extremely graceful. He was a typical American who had developed a Roman second nature. As I started to draw, he continued dictating letters to his secretary:

"Dear Countess—How happy I am to learn that your daughter—fill in name—is becoming the bride of such a promising—comma—charming young man—semicolon—blessings—yours sincerely—no—devotedly."

"My dear Bishop—It is most unfortunate that during the current year we cannot accept—the long waiting list.—However, if next year the application on behalf—*alinea*—Yours in Christ."

"Oh, here is that letter from that poor soul in Iowa. Wait just a moment—"

"She calls me 'Director of Bishops!' " He smiled. "Look, let us send her a medal of Pope John. Poor lonely soul," he repeated, the light-blue eyes all at once looking compassionate. The Archbishop got up and bent over a drawer full of medals. "No," he muttered, "this is the Sacred Heart—this is Pius XII, isn't that something! This is Holy Year—ah, here we are!"

With the medal he walked back to his desk, sat down, and looked up at the deep-blue sky through the window for inspiration: "Dear Mrs. McGinnis—" It grew into a very kind, lengthy letter to that poor old lonely soul somewhere in Iowa.

A seminarian came in. He had organized the chartering of planes for six hundred relatives of priests to be ordained. The Rector complimented the young man on a recent sermon, and when he had left said, before continuing his dictation: "He is a good boy! He is also a fine organizer and has business sense and mental balance. That's what counts. That and perseverance."

"—and I should urge Your Excellency, without wishing to interfere in any way—" The blue eyes were steely now.

When I had finished, he invited me to sketch at the College the following Sunday, when the five American cardinals would be his guests. That Sunday, while I was sketching their Eminences during a walk in the park of the College, Cardinal Cushing spotted me.

"Hi, there, my artist friend!" he cried out. Then suddenly he frowned: "So you came anyway, did you?"

"Your Eminence was overruled," I said, pulling Pope John's medal from my pocket. Cushing's face can change in a second from a formidable mask to something very loveable: "Isn't that wonderful!" he beamed.

When Tenente Martelli called early Wednesday morning he sounded genuinely sorry. "We got a reply to your request to Cardinal Masella," he said, *"Je suis affolé,* but he absolutely refused. He says you can take photographs, but no drawings—"

So this was *aggiornamento* as understood by the "conservatives." At this twenty-first Ecumenical Council after Christ, by special dispensation of the Cardinal-Chamberlain, photographers were allowed and artists were anathema. "Get thee behind me, Raphael!" Could the Cardinal-Chamberlain be a philistine notwithstanding that noble, fascinating head I liked to draw? I asked myself over a lonely espresso. Still, he was the boss during the *sede vacante.* There must be other ways. After all, it was now proven that the Church was not the homogenized monolith all had assumed.

The pressroom during this period was not the well-appointed one on the Via della Conciliazione with its United Nations atmosphere. During the Council I had made my contacts there. That was closed now; instead, at the offices of the *Osservatore Romano,* a dingy room had been set apart for the press. It was an oblong room that had not been painted for twenty years at least. At a few tables bored journalists were discussing the *papabili* endlessly. It did not resemble an international press center so much as it did the back room of a run-down police station where complainants are kept waiting. The office of Signor Mazzini must have been upstairs. The second in command sat in a dingy room on the ground floor with a flimsy door made impregnable by the presence of an important personage called Antonio, an athletic-looking movie-Italian, who, in contrast with other Vatican officials, wore a blue-and-white-striped polo shirt over his wrestler's torso. One of his functions was certainly that of janitor. But he was also obviously used by the journalists as a source of inside information; at any rate, he acted as if he could distribute privileges. Antonio, who had at first eyed me with the disapproval he held for newcomers in general, and foreigners in particular, had thawed probably because of my attitude of respect and indestructible, cheerful courtesy. He advised me to apply to Monsignor Primo Principi—"through someone important."

Tenente Martelli of The
Gendarmería Pontifica

I did. No reply came. In my notebook, however, I found the name of a Father Herron, treasurer of the Congregation of Missionaries of Sons of the Immaculate Heart of Mary, also called the Claretian Fathers. I decided to take the long taxi ride to the Via del Sacre Core di Maria, and was lucky. Father Herron could help me! He sent his fat Neapolitan assistant with me to Cardinal Larraona, Prefect of the Sacred Congregation of Rites, who is also Cardinal Protector of the Claretian Fathers.

Cardinal Larraona lives in one of those modern elevator buildings off the Via della Conciliazione. A tiny young Spanish nun who looked like an El Greco madonna opened the door. The reception room was Vatican-modern. In a corner a large plaster madonna was standing on a cream-puff cloud; a painting of Jesus in Arabic head-dress stared at me. There was also a religious picture made of butter-fly wings that changed metallic colors according to the point of viewing and a Chinese landscape painted on velvet. On the table lay an album of the Cardinal's latest visit to Chicago: smiling midwestern ladies in bejeweled glasses and flower hats surrounding a tall man with heavy features and lively eyes.

The Cardinal was out. But his secretary, a young and charming red-cheeked Spaniard, Father Ruiz, proved very helpful. A letter would go off to Archbishop Primo Principi forthwith. I was called a day later. The letter had already been answered; the request had been granted. The Archbishop had said O.K.

He said it as follows:

YOUR MOST REVEREND EMINENCE:

I have the honor to confirm receipt of your most Venerated letter, in which your Most Reverend Eminence has recommended Signor Frederick Franck, who desires to execute some drawings in the Vatican Basilica.

I am pleased to inform You, having already arranged it, that the afore-mentioned gentleman may have free access for the purpose described by Your Eminence.

I am very happy to have been of service to Your Eminence and I eagerly profit from this opportunity to express to You the respectful obedience in which I bow down to kiss the Sacred Purple, and profess myself,

> Your Most Reverend Eminence's
> most unique, most devoted,
> most obedient servant,
>
> χ P. PRINCIPI

Father Ruiz was to meet me at Tenente Martelli's office to make it all official. He was dressed in purple silk and his pink face was all smiles. Martelli and his assistant were also smiling happily. "Wonderful!" the lieutenant congratulated me. "I am so glad for you."

"Will you give me a written permit to show the guards?" I asked.

"Oh," said Martelli, "that won't be necessary. Just go ahead." This seemed overoptimistic. I expected endless arguments with the detectives. Better start right away! I walked with my sketchbook toward St. Peter's. "Just call headquarters," I rehearsed in Italian. "I have the permission. Just call headquarters. I have the permission." Ten minutes later I passed the triple guard at the main door of the Basilica. I had my sketchbook demonstratively open with a pencil clipped to it. "Just call headquarters," I rehearsed again under my breath. But nobody stopped me at the entrance. The plainclothes guards, standing at every ten steps or so inside the Basilica, pretended not to see me. Had I become invisible? I did a quick sketch of a side chapel to test further. No reaction. Did they work with telepathy?

At the Confession Altar, benches had been placed to barricade the space beyond, where a ceremonial catafalque was being built. I sat on one of the benches and started to sketch. The detectives apparently did not notice me. I climbed over it. I was still invisible. I shall never know how it worked, but there must be something rather efficient about the work of this friendly Martelli and his organization. The only explanation I could imagine was that Martelli had telephoned to Guard A: "Baldheaded fellow with sketchbook absolutely kosher. Do not disturb." And A walked his ten steps to B and repeated it, and within ten minutes the whole Vatican knew about the baldheaded fellow with the sketchbook! . . .

Ara Coeli, as it is called, or "Santa Maria Ara Coeli," is the Basilica of the City of Rome. It means "Gates of Heaven." It is a long steep climb up the Capitoline hill to this Altar of Heaven, along an enormous, breath-taking stone staircase. Somewhere halfway up, the twins Romulus and Remus are being suckled by the she-wolf. In the big black-draped church the Requiem Mass to be celebrated on behalf of the municipality of Rome in memory of Pope John had not yet started. I was an hour early. The hundreds of crystal chandeliers had not yet been lit, and the mournful afternoon light filtered through the windows, transforming the crystals into myriads of dull tears. I was alone in the hot church with an excited, disturbed-looking, emaciated man in rags, who carried a bouquet of roses. He knelt at all the side altars and slunk around the empty ceremonial catafalque, unable to decide where to deposit his flowers. At last he sat down close to where I was, with the roses on his knees, and sank deeply into prayer. His face became radiant in ecstasy.

A detachment of policemen in snow-white uniforms arrived. The official in charge, stiff in his frock coat, started to rush to and fro excitedly, with all the stereotyped ceremonial gestures of head and arms that symbolize efficient organization. In the oppressive heat he wore spats and gloves. One policeman one step to the right. No, not quite. A little farther back. *Ecco!*—A smile. Next policeman to the right of the door. A wave of the gloved hand to correct the position.— *Ecco!* Honor guards in Renaissance uniforms entered, were positioned to flank the altar—the throne of the Apostolic Nuncio was moved a shade forward—fine!

The church filled up and the little gilt chairs with purple cushions set around the catafalque were occupied. It remained very still, warm, and sleepy. The ladies and gentlemen sat on their chairs and looked somehow Episcopalian. The Mayor of Rome entered, flanked by more Renaissance figures and high-ranking cops in gala black-and-gold. The mayor had a big belly in his freshly pressed dark suit; across it, he wore the Italian tricolor. The Apostolic Nuncio, senescent and very frail, sat nodding on his throne. As the Mass began, only the police inspector was still rushing about, gesturing like a demented orchestra conductor. At the *Domine, non sum dignus*, the wild-eyed man with the flowers ran to the altar rail and knelt. A few women followed. Nobody had counted on this; hurriedly, resentfully, communion was given. The celebrating monsignor gave the absolution and sprinkled the catafalque with holy water and incense. It had been a cold, short ceremony, this Mass that had been announced all over Rome on big posters: *"Cittadini, Romani!"* it started. The citizens, the Romans were not really present here—nor was Pope John's spirit.

The first six of the Requiem Masses to be celebrated as part of the Novemdiali took place in the Canons' Chapel near the entrance of Saint Peter's. A memorial catafalque had been built in the center of the Chapel, surrounded by the twenty candles that symbolize the *Lux Eterna*. The first celebrant was Monsignor Felici, the muscular Secretary General of the Second Vatican Council. No cardinals would be present until the last three solemn Masses that close the funeral ceremonies for a deceased pope. The ceremonies in the Chapel gave the impression of a rite performed without much inner necessity. In their dark pews the eighteen canons in fur stoles went through the liturgy routinely and, except when the choir enveloped them in the ecstatic music of Carissimi or Palestrina, they looked like dried-out judges in a dusty courtroom, seen in a dream. The Master of Ceremonies was a small man with impressive movements who was clearly enjoying himself. He seemed to delight in pointing up the slightest mistakes, sending priests and acolytes back from the altar and with imperial movements of his hands commanding them to approach a

. . . in the Sacristy of St. Peter's

second time, this time a little more to the center, a shade more to the right. He held his little round head with gray wiry hair at a slight angle and the thin mouth was pulled into an ironic semismile that stayed fixed as if drawn in hard pencil. He fascinated me. With his old-fashioned face of a priestly professional he epitomized the Canon's Chapel. The Roman people kneeling at the entrance of the Chapel were exalted amateurs. Was this a dying church paying homage to the empty catafalque of the man who had reawakened it elsewhere—in the hearts of the living? The cold, tired eyes of the canons sometimes suddenly widened as they glanced in astonishment to where such fervent singing rose from the people at their Chapel's door.

I was beginning to feel at home in St. Peter's. I felt I had learned to imitate successfully that particular way of walking and looking that characterized the in-group: a bit solemn, a bit unconcerned, as if you might be whistling quietly to yourself without relaxing your church face. Sometimes I sensed that a plainclothesman might still feel unsure about me as I walked into the sacristy with a sketchpad under my arm. But then at the critical moment I always met one of the gendarmes I knew and immediately went through the ritual of hearty handshaking, showing a sketch or two, and in general giving a demonstration of being persona grata. By now I had been given the title *Professore,* which the gendarmes used with Italian enthusiasm. All the cops around, from the spidery little mean ones to the big bullies with Neanderthal eyebrows, were becoming smiling, servile accomplices. In the sacristy I met Cardinal Tappouni's assistant, Bishop Mansourati, who stood there talking to the *Ceremoniarius* I had just seen in the Canon's Chapel. I was introduced. Monsignore Arturo Coletti was all smiles.

"I should like to draw you too, Monsignore. I saw you in the Canon's Chapel." The little man made abject gestures of humility. "Oh, not me," he said in his comical, staccato French. "I am not important enough and I have no face."

"On the contrary, Your Excellency, you impressed me very much and, if I may say so, you have a most distinguished ecclesiastical expression." He giggled like an old girl now and we made an appointment for the next day.

"*Au revoir, cher professeur,*" he said, "*et mes hommages à Madame.*" His face was indeed marvelous. It had dignity, skepticism, humor and had been chiseled by a lifetime of professional piety, subtle flattery, ever alert diplomacy. I had never mentioned that I was married, but since Monsignore Coletti ended every conversation with this "hommages à Madame," I assumed he was convinced this was the most elegant way to end a conversation in French, and that he probably repeated it routinely, whether saying good-bye to journalists, generals, or archbishops.

I saw the Sacristy of St. Peter's as a meeting place, a clubhouse, and a dressing room, a bit like the lobby of the United States Senate: cardinals, archbishops, young priests milled around, introductions were made, pious old ladies from prominent families, prim faces at their holiest, stood around and waited for hours to have a chance to kiss the ring of their favorite bishop. Recalcitrant choirboys were berated by choirmasters. Groups of decrepit canons huddled together to air the latest gossip and scattered obsequiously when cardinals returned from celebrating Mass in vestments stiff with gold embroidery.

Suddenly a sobbing little girl in first-communion dress, a candle in her hand, appeared from behind an ancient cardinal with his trainbearer, searching for her mother. A bishop with a nose like a strawberry was trying unsuccessfully to escape from a veiled, long-toothed aristocratic hag. Plainclothesmen in charge came to look at my drawing, but with newfound self-assurance I waved them

Msgr. Arturo Coletti

. . . Cardinal Masella celebrating Requiem Mass

away. Chiseled in stone in large characters was the word SILEN-
TIUM. It did not deaden the constant din.

I spent the last three days of the Novemdiale in St. Peter's at the
Requiem Masses, at which cardinals—Ferrato, Doepfner, Alfrink,
Suenens, Cigognani—were officiating, their faces now familiar. Once
the lights went on the Basilica became radiant, yet only when the
Sistine Chapel Choir began singing did the building really come
alive. St. Peter's has to be experienced in a sea of music, waves
rising against the columns, ebbing away through the archways, eddy-
ing around the gilded cosmos of the Bernini altar. As the boys'
voices rise the eye must be carried on those waves of Palestrina to the
radiance of the dove of the Holy Spirit, high above the papal throne.

The huge catafalque, like a rather vulgar birthday cake bristling
with candles, was a pyramid of candle flames against dull black and
gold. It was topped with an empty coffin crowned by a tiara. It was
so high and far away that it looked like a baby's coffin. We sat around
it dressed in our violet and purple and scarlet silk and moiré, our

gold-embroidered tunics, our tailcoats, our striped trousers, our plain cassocks, our lace rochets, our stiff embroidered vestments to mourn the dead man, saluting him with our drawn swords, our damascened halberds—as in all funeral ceremonies, seeing ourselves as normally alive, him as exceptionally dead, not even here realizing our transiency, in this Basilica where all the living and the dying and the long-dead were perceptibly united in irrevocable partnership.

At the last Mass of the Novemdiale, traditionally the most solemn of the Requiem Masses, the entire diplomatic corps was present and the highest aristocracy of Italy and of the Church was on hand to enhance this spectacle of Renaissance splendor, to honor this Pope John who had said: "We must shake off the imperial dust that has gathered on the throne of Peter since Constantine"; who had said: "Always to be in contact with the self-styled great of this world and to be saddened by the smallness of their spirit, where the supernatural is concerned." Or again: "This morning I must receive cardinals, princes, and important government representatives. But this afternoon I want to spend some time with ordinary people, who have no other title than their dignity of being human and children of God." And also: "The Church is not an archaeological museum, but the antique fountain which gives water to the generations of today as it has done to those of the past."

I took up my post at the side entrance, where the highest dignitaries were entering. It was like a procession of ghosts. Above the door, as part of the monument of Pope Alexander IV a stone skeleton hovered over the vain parade. Cardinal Valerio Valente—he died a few weeks afterward—was being fussed over by chamberlains. The Duke of Bergamo shuffled in, senile and trembling in his fancy dress. They stumbled in on their unsteady legs, these old counts and dukes, these judges of the Rota, Knights of Malta and of the Holy Sepulcher, loaded down by their medals and chains of office. The Swiss guards stood at attention and saluted the little old men who straightened up pathetically, attempting to stick out their decorated chests, carrying their tremulous heads high in the gold-embroidered stiff collars of their gala finery.

Then three women entered; noble ushers scrambled to get to them first. Bows, so carefully weighed here and adjusted in depth according to rank, went to their deepest ninety-degree angles. "La Duchesse d'Aosta," an old French monsignor next to me whispered. "La

... then three women entered ...

Princesse Maria Gabriella." The Duchess looked carnivorous and angry, impatiently pounding the stone floor with her black-and-silver cane. At her side the former queen of Bulgaria, her chest covered with the commander's crosses of defunct orders, looked haggard and desperate in her long black dress, the huge mantilla framing a face lined with frustration.

So this was the woman who once married King Boris and was going to have that Roman Catholic wedding! Had not Boris promised Monsignor Roncalli solemnly that theirs would be a Catholic ceremony? And Roncalli had obtained dispensation from the Vatican for this mixed Catholic-Orthodox union. Then Boris reneged; he had an Orthodox marriage ceremony right afterward, for which Roncalli was blamed. "He cheated me," Roncalli commented in 1930, "but we have to live and seek peace. What a misery this human life! Let us pray for him."

And now no more Boris, no more Roncalli, just this old, frustrated, lonely woman, walking into St. Peter's, bowed to by chamberlains, acknowledged by guards presenting arms, her wilted chest plastered with obsolete trinkets, only here still Queen of Bulgaria, a ghost among ghosts.

I stood there at the entrance amidst the *commendatori* and *cavalieri* and drew. The choir had started and it was too late to get up on one of the tribunes, so I wandered around through passages. I stood next to Cardinal Gerlier and drew the hawklike Archbishop of Lyon, who had acted so bravely against the Nazis that a French fascist paper had written: "I demand the head of Gerlier, cardinal, delirious Talmudist, traitor to his faith, his country and his race."

As I began to draw Agagianian who was sitting next to him, a chamberlain in his white ruffle snarled at me: "You cannot draw here." I stared at him through my precious monocle—the more effective the more snobbish its target—and snarled back: "I beg your pardon!" going on imperturbably. In the wings the General of the Noble Guard had sunk down on a bench, his man-of-distinction face pale and perspiring. Next to him an ancient prelate was gasping for breath and Commendatore Giovanni, the Chief Usher, slouched in exhaustion after all this bowing in of royalty. The Soviet-Russian

Cardinals Gerlier and Agagianian

observer, the Archimandrite Vladimir Kotliarov, stopped a moment to let me draw him.

In a corner, Swiss guards had stealthily taken off their plumed helmets and were mopping the sweat from their young faces and talking in Swiss dialect about scooters and cameras. They stood leaning on their halberds, talking, joking, and boasting. They did not belong to the ghosts; they were only disguised to resemble them.

I sneaked behind the main altar and stood in the back row of the Tribuna Santa Elena. Opposite me Cardinal Tisserant was sitting like an old heraldic lion. His head was thrown back, the square wide beard stood defiantly horizontal, challenging death. They were all men in their eighties: Fossato of Turin, who sat next to him, thin and shrunken, his narrow white face with the prominent lower lip expressionless. Cardinal Pizzardo, a worried, suspicious, emaciated man, sat hunched in his mountain of purple. Only the Cardinal-Chamberlain Masella throned erect like a king; the long eyelids hooded the haughty feudal eyes; the mouth was frozen in a nearly imperceptible curve that might express benevolence, displeasure, amusement, or irony.

After this final Requiem Mass I walked into Trastevere and sat in front of one of those bars where the working people of Rome have

Cardinals Tisserant, Masella, Pizzardo, Fossato

their coffee. The contrast made me start drawing again. Rome, I noticed, had become St. Peter's for me, but here I suddenly realized that the city had gone on living and sweating, making love and money, rushing around in its buses and miniscule cars, only now and then thinking about its beloved Pope John and talking about his successor. "We'll never get a pope like that again!" was the usual conclusion.

In St. Peter's at last, they had done with Pope John. His body lay safely deep in the crypt of the Basilica under a ton of granite. For nine days the ceremonial above him had continued in order to push him out of our consciousness. "There is nothing so dead as a dead pope," people repeated. The preparation for the Conclave that would choose John's successor had been going on for a fortnight, and behind a façade made of black crêpe and the violet silk of mourning, influences and power centers were already bitterly engaged in battle.

On the café terrace in Trastevere, while earning my seat by drinking coffee, lemonades, and camparis, I sat for hours and held my own memorial service.

In my portfolio I had notes on the sayings of Pope John, culled from conversations, magazines, and newspapers. I started to read and to savor them again one by one. To me all his anecdotes were parables he could tell in non-ecclesiastical language. They have been repeated often by now, but they are worth it!

"The representative of the highest spiritual authority on earth is glad and even proud to be the son of a humble but robust laborer."

Someone asked him a favor he could not grant: *"Sorry, but I am only the Pope."*

To the prisoners in Regina Coeli he said: *"Since you couldn't come to me, I had to come to you."* One of them asked him: "Do those words of hope you have spoken also apply to me, who am so great a sinner?" The Pope, as a reply, opened his arms and embraced him.

"I don't see why I should eat alone. I feel like a punished seminarian. I have carefully read the gospel and haven't found a passage prescribing that I should eat alone. Jesus, as you know, liked to eat in company."

To a ten-year-old boy who had written him that he wasn't sure whether he wanted to become a policeman or a pope, he wrote: *"Learn to become a policeman . . . as far as being a pope is concerned . . . anybody can become a pope. The proof is that I have become one. When you come to Rome, come and see me. I'll gladly talk it over with you."*

About the Communists: *"They are the enemies of the Church, but the Church has no enemies."*

"Isn't it often painful to have to live with certain colleagues who talk about nothing but the exterior form of priestly activities, who have so much trouble to repress in their hearts a thirst and search— not even modest or veiled—for promotion, climbing, distinction; who have taken the habit to interpret everything in a minor key, preparing themselves in this way for a precocious old age of dryness and squeamishness."

"I have never blushed about my earthly family, simple and modest as they may be: that is its real title of nobility. I have sometimes helped it in its modest urgent need, as a poor man helps other poor men, but without pulling it out of its poverty, which is its happiness and its joy."

When asked what he would like best to do after the Council was finished: *"Spend a whole day with my brothers, working in the fields."*

At a banquet, where he was sitting next to an elegant lady in particularly deep décolletage, he insisted that she eat an apple for dessert. As she seemed astonished, Monsignor Roncalli said: *"But please eat it, Madame; after all it was only after Eve had eaten the apple that she noticed that she was naked."*

Why didn't he preside over the Council personally during the first session? *"If I had been there, would you have felt yourselves quite as free? Would you have had the courage, for instance, to applaud when the President interrupted Cardinal Ottaviani during his intervention? And if you had done so, wouldn't you all have looked at me to see what kind of a face I made? True or not?"*

When he overheard someone remarking, "Isn't he fat?" he turned around and said: *"Don't you know, Madame, that a conclave is not a beauty contest?"*

"There are only two ways to be a good diplomat," the Pope said, *"either to be as mute as a mole, or talkative to the point where what you are saying loses all importance. Since I am an Italian, I prefer the second method."*

"I do not ask tourists to wear furs and woollen garments in Italy. They can wear that modern, fresh, and soft American silk that is a real refrigerator and inexpensive. On the other hand, Italy is not on the equator, and even on the equator don't the lions wear their fur and the crocodiles their so precious skins?"

To chattering women during an audience: *"If you are not quiet, I'll have to bless you right away and go back to my apartment."*

Waking up in the middle of the night, plagued by a problem, John XXIII said to himself: *"I'll talk it over with the Pope."* Then with a shock he realized: *"But I am the Pope."* *"All right, then,"* he concluded, *"I'll have to talk to our Lord."*

He also told that when he was terribly worried about a decision, he would say to himself: *"Stop worrying, Angelo. You're not that important."*

"These contacts with the crowds, these audiences—oh, what consolation!"

During a visit to the Hospital of the Holy Spirit, the Mother Superior, all confused, introduced herself: "Holy Father, I am the Superior of the Holy Spirit." *"Well, aren't you lucky,"* responded the Pope. *"I am only the Vicar of Jesus Christ."*

All this is full of wit and kindness and seems to confirm the imperfect image of John XXIII as "good old Pope John," the man who could say to an audience: *"We shall pray for you and for your families. Pray also for your pope, for, to be honest, let me say to you, I hope to live long. I love life."*

He loved life, but he did not find it easy: *"Sadness often tries to invade Our spirit,"* he said on Easter, 1961. *"To see the violence with which anti-Christian error spreads, the insanities which flood the world in ideas about 'the good life' up to the point where innumerable mortals are persuaded that the heavens are empty and that there is nothing else for man than to enjoy the earthly paradise. . . ."*

Christmas, 1960: *"Are we not often, yes, too often, face to face with a shameless and insolent anti-Decalogue?"*

Again he sounded deadly sad when in January, 1959, he said to the faithful: *"We tell you in all confidence that the usual serenity of spirit which shows on our face and which rejoices our sons, hides the laceration and desolation of our soul."*

About the press he complained, on August 12, 1959: *"It is not love of knowledge, of culture, or of truth which guides some pens, but the unhealthy fire of certain passions, the measureless desire for notoriety and gain, which denies the irrepressible appeals of conscience."*

Only later in his pontificate, when taken up in the torrent of his own great work, did his optimism break through and could he declare his *"complete disagreement with those prophets of doom who always announce catastrophes."*

To the journalists he said (3/24/61): *"We want to be and are above all in the service of truth. You, too, gentlemen, desire this and it is the honor of your profession."*

"We are not the victims of an illusion; and the Spirit of Truth, of Union, of Concord, of Peace, always hovers over this world and stretches its wings over our heads in order to wake in us the same wonder which at the beginning of time made the entire Universe palpitate with a new life."

It was his conviction *"that men, dear brothers, are all on the way that leads to Christ; many, very many, unconsciously. . . ."* (5/1/62)

In *Mater et Magistra* he says: *"Our era is invaded and penetrated by fundamental errors. Yet it is also an era which opens to the Church immense possibilities for doing good. . . . What matters is to help men so that their time on earth be less sad."* (5/30/62)

He bids his priests *"hold themselves to what is most simple and most ancient in the practice of the Church."* He does not believe in *"little sentimental effusions,"* but reminds his priests that *"the people ask from us the substantial bread of truth"* (10/2/59), and that *"profession of Christian faith cannot be reduced to inscription in registers. It must before all create a new man"* (in *Princeps pastorum*).

Interior of St. Peter's with Cardinal Alfrink

As time goes on, a supernatural optimism, founded on his unshakable confidence in God and his mission suffuses his every word and gesture: *"In the present state of things, Providence guides us toward a new order in human relations which, through the works of men and often beyond their very expectations, is oriented toward the accomplishment of its unexpected and supreme designs, and everything, even human diversity, works together to the greatest good of the Church"* (11/10/62).

Little did it matter to him that he might not see the end of his work: *"This great enterprise to which we have consecrated ourselves [the Council] what does it matter whether our eyes may see its development and its conclusion? It is enough for the confident serenity of our soul to have responded with simplicity to this happy inspiration and to be ready to do all and dare all for its success* (11/13/60). Catholic, non-Catholic, faithful or heretic, it did not seem to matter to him. He was "the gardener of the world, but, rather than weeding, he watered what was growing."

About an unbeliever: *"Well, what separates us? Our ideas . . . you have to admit that that does not amount to much. . . ."*

To John, the Church had no charter to dominate the world; its function was to serve. He called himself "the servant of the servants of God" and he meant what he said. Who would ever have believed that in this twentieth century a pope would die and the whole world would sit in wake? It could be this man only who said to the Archbishop of Cambrai, pointing to the Crucifix on his table: *"If you knew how I suffer because so many men believe that the Church condemns them. I do as He does, I open my arms and I love."*
And who could say to a delegation of American Jews, with his great smile and his great openness: *"See, I am Joseph, your brother."*

Here ended my private memorial service on the terrace of a café in Trastevere.

It was all over now. Next day I would be drawing the rooms of the Conclave, the Sistine Chapel, and listening to all the authoritative forecasts, reading all about the glamorized lives of the *papabili*. On Wednesday the Conclave would begin.

On Tuesday, June 18, 1963, I stood waiting in the courtyard of San Damaso at the top of the Regal Staircase. Radio Televisione Italiana trucks were being unloaded; sixty photographers were assembling big cameras and strobo-flashes; journalists were sitting on the fenders of cardinals' Mercedes cars, placing bets on the outcome of the Conclave. Workingmen in old gray dusters were lugging heavy gilded chairs, beds and wardrobes across the little square. The rooms of the Conclave were still being furnished. Carpenters were putting up the wooden barriers and adjusting the turnstiles. Gendarmes in tricornered hats were watching them lazily in the sun. When Tenente Martelli appeared, two tall Americans, loaded with cameras, intercepted him. They had just arrived by plane, they explained, to take pictures for the New York *Daily Mirror*. No, they had not made any arrangements for special permission.

Martelli was making his official face of "nothing doing," but as usual he relented a bit later. He was just too human and benevolent to keep this expression for long. You could see him think again: "The poor devils have to make their living." "But, please," he was saying, pointing at their sport shirts, "put on decent suits, this is not a baseball game!" From then on, the *Daily Mirror* men could be seen in rented tuxedos morning, noon, and night.

The guided tour started. First to the cardinals' cells. These may be called "cells" during the Conclave, but actually most of these temporary dwellings of cardinals are elegant drawing rooms or suites with treasures of antique furniture, paintings, and perhaps some bits of decoration by such muralists as Raphael. The most luxurious cell was the first one we were shown. It had been reserved for Cardinal Mindszenty in case at the last minute he should decide to come.

The photographers went to work taking angle shots, standing on chairs and photographing every detail of the bed, the desk, the crucifix on the night-table.

They found a little, bare bedroom where an iron bedstead was standing and at the sight of this they sighed with relief. For in the traditional journalism of Conclaves, the cardinals have to sleep most uncomfortably in dark storerooms, drafty passages, and above all in creaking iron beds. In reality, the little iron bedstead was meant for the cardinal's secretary or *conclavista*.

I wandered away and into the drawing room of Monsignor Van Lierde, already transformed into a cell, where a bearded archbishop was sitting on a gilded rococo settee reading his *Osservatore Romano*. In a hallway an old monsignor, majestically seated on a displaced throne, hoped desperately to be photographed at last. In the *Sala Regia,* whistling carpenters were hammering away, building a ramp to cover some steps over which the poor old shuffling cardinals might have stumbled and broken their hips. In the kitchen of the Conclave the vaulted empty space was filled with brand-new refrigerators and ranges. The photographers were disheartened. Refrigerators are not photogenic. I drew the kitchen, disguising the disgruntled photographers as chefs, only to find later that there would be not chefs but nuns to do the cooking!

In the Sistine Chapel I drew the famous little stove and the boxes of straw bottle-jackets that would make the smoke. The Chapel was dark and dull. Workmen were still adjusting the *baldacchinos* over the cardinals' thrones, for they had to function well; only the one above the throne of the newly elected pope would be allowed to stay up after his election. The man from the *Daily Mirror,* focusing his lens on the "Last Judgment," said angrily: "What do they expect you to do in this light? And is *this* the famous sixteenth Chapel? That's the only one I have to get; that's the one they're interested in. What's it used for, anyway?"

One group of dispirited photographers had sat down on the cardinals' thrones yawning; others were standing in the center of the Chapel, talking or shooting at Michelangelo's "Christ" with flashbulbs. I drew them, disguising them in scarlet, flowing robes. After all, it would be just like that next day after the first ballot: cardinals standing around, lobbying for their candidates.

"How on earth did you get into the Conclave?" Cardinal Bea was to exclaim later when I showed him the drawing.

The *Mirror* man said enviously: "For you it's easy!" And he stayed with me as we walked through the endless Borgia apartments, visiting more cells. He was intrigued by a Renaissance saddle on an antique stand and started to take pictures of it. Then he squatted on his haunches, looking under the saddle for a switch to make it canter. He shook his head admiringly: "Ain't that something, how they're trying to keep the old boys fit."

In the dining room, workmen were putting chairs into position with a great show of haste. Collections of spears, swords, and shields decorated the walls; marble busts of popes and cardinals watched us from above. Two mustached older workmen were sitting down, mimicking conversing cardinals daintily spooning soup. But in the room where in 1958 Angelo Roncalli had slept during the Conclave that elected him a hush fell over the photographers, and whatever they said was said in whispers.

In the emptiness of the *sede vacante* anything seemed possible. Predictions flew around. Would the next pope continue the Council? Would he continue it sincerely, or only bow to public opinion and then quietly neutralize or even sabotage its purpose, in order to create at any rate a pause in this dizzying forward surge of the Church into the world? Would he be an Italian? Or perhaps an Italianized foreigner, like Agagianian? Or a progressive like Cardinal Koenig of Vienna or Suenens of Belgium or Alfrink of Holland? Or would it after all be Montini, who had been mentioned all the time? Hadn't he been rumored to be co-author with Pope John of the now famous opening statement of the Council? Had he not been the only guest of the Pope to stay in the Apostolic Palace during the Council's first session? Hadn't he been silent during the debates at the Pope's bidding in order not to show his hand too much? Or would it be Lercaro from Bologna, who was most like Pope John in character? Or perhaps a middle-of-the-road man like Urbani, who like Pope John had been Patriarch of Venice? Or perhaps a Ferreto or Confalioneri? Or an arch-conservative like Antoniutti? Would he be a thin man after a fat one, as popular belief would have it? Or, according to the twelfth-century prophecy of Malachi, an Irish bishop whose prophecies were published in 1595, would he be the "flower of flowers"? There were lilies in the coats of arms of Roberti, Siri, Wiszynski and—Montini!

Would it be a long conclave or a short one?

The skeptics in my favorite espresso bar felt that in this heat it could only be short: "Otherwise the old boys would die like flies." If it was very short, they said, one could be sure that it would be Montini, who already had forty votes sewn up.

But at the end of all the forecasts someone would inevitably repeat the old saw: "He who enters the Conclave a pope comes out a cardinal."

The Mass of the Holy Spirit

On the morning of Wednesday, June 19, I sat on the Tribuna Sant'Elena and drew St. Peter's as the Mass of the Holy Spirit was celebrated by Cardinal Tisserant, Dean of the Sacred College of Cardinals, in a Basilica aglow with light, expectation, and Palestrina's music. After the Mass, the Secretary of the Briefs to Princes, Monsignor Tondini, delivered the traditional speech *"De Eligendo Pontifica"* ("For the Election of the Sovereign Pontiff"), in which he had to impress on his audience, according to canon law, the gravity of its responsibility, and to formulate wishes for the next pontificate. It was an endless, droning, and somber speech in elegant Latin.

In his anything but tactful allocution Monsignor Tondini told the princes of the Church that not all the applause for the defunct pope had come from people "who believe in the real values of the Spirit and in the dogmatic teaching and morals of the Church." In barely veiled criticism of Pope John, he stressed the necessity to "reestablish the supernatural virtues in the lives of Christians," and as much as ordered Their Eminences to elect a pope who would postpone the continuation of the Council until a "suitable time," counseling them the "greatest prudence" after the audacities of John XXIII.

That afternoon at five o'clock I stood in the hall between the Pauline Chapel and the Sistine Chapel, overfilled with dignitaries and journalists. Desperately I tried to draw the cardinals filing into the Conclave. Outside the heat was unbearable, but here in the glare of television lights and the nauseating pressure of human bodies it was sheer torture. How could I draw in this stiff black suit, pushed right, left, and back by these bemedaled men, forced with them into this too-small space, each intent on not missing a face or a gesture?

Still, I kept scribbling on my paper without being able to see what I was scribbling. I drew the diplomats forming an honor guard opposite me and then, trying to protect my sketchbook from pushing elbows, a little emaciated cardinal as he walked in. The cardinals walked past me and the choir sang *Veni, Creator Spiritus.* Suenens, Spellman, Frings strode past with appropriately solemn faces. Cardinal Brown of Ireland looked more forbidding than ever. Only Cushing had a slightly ironic smile.

. . . at the entrance of the Conclave

Then I saw Montini. He was walking as if in a trance, unseeing, his face deeply lined, a man turned inward, stooped as if a great weight pressed him down. My hand started to draw: In the place I had left open in my sketch because there was no space to turn my page, as in a trance, I scribbled Cardinal Montini, walking into the Conclave from which he would emerge Pope!

At six o'clock I stood waiting at one of the gates of the Conclave for Prince Chigi who—in accordance with centuries of tradition—would lock the gates and isolate the eighty cardinals and their staff from the world until a pope was chosen.

Trucks making last-minute deliveries of lettuce, soap powder, and butter were still driving into the Conclave. Haughty wives of Noble Guards were impatiently stamping their high heels while waiting for their husbands, suffering and sweating under their mantillas. A decrepit old meddlesome canon in purple biretta was giving orders to everybody, and was obeyed by no one. He looked like an angry chicken with his red, unblinking eyes. When a detachment of Swiss guards marched out of the gates, he refused to make way and was bumped into by every passing guard. They made him turn about on his axis like a mechanical toy, the angry eyes glaring and the high voice protesting.

The Palatine guard, short stocky men like streetcar conductors in gala attire, dribbled through the gates, and then the Noble Guards marched out in thigh-high patent-leather boots, black-and-gold horsetailed helmets hiding their eyes. They paused to talk to their women, kissing hands and clicking spurred heels together in order to bask a few more moments in the glory of their fancy dress. Then they disappeared into a dressing room, to emerge again as harmless fellows, paunches no longer contained by leather belts, stooped shoulders no longer heightened by epaulets, bald heads no longer hidden beneath Roman helmets.

Soon after six, Prince Chigi appeared with his retinue. Small, a frail septuagenarian, birdlike in his Renaissance finery, he fumbled

Cardinal Montini entering the Conclave

for minutes with his big key, refusing to put on his glasses in his moment of glory. Chigi looked princely and mysterious; the cameras flashed. Would he be there for the next Conclave and be once more for a full fiftieth of a second the center of world attention?

All next day St. Peter's Square was black with people. In the space reserved for photographers, platforms had been built from which they were spying at the windows of the Vatican Palace, hoping for something to happen. At one moment a cardinal, forgetting himself, opened the window and smoked a cigarette. The tele-objectives started a barrage and got their cardinal. Once in the morning of that Thursday, once in the evening, black smoke poured out of the comical stovepipe, sticking up atop the Sistine Chapel. It looked white at first, then became blacker and blacker as people were checking with their transistors how black it really was.

On Friday morning it was again very hot. Everybody was convinced that nothing could happen until nightfall. I sat on the sidewalk of the Via della Conciliazione, drawing the crowd. Then, at 11:22 A.M. another puff of white smoke wafted into the blue sky.

"E bianco!" a great shout went up. As the smoke kept on pouring out, whiter and whiter, a senseless excitement seemed to get hold of everybody. Within minutes, from nowhere at all, great mobs suddenly surged through the Via della Conciliazione to St. Peter's Square: thousands of nuns, tourists, seminarians, old priests in berets, long-skirted peasant women from the provinces. In the Square the sun was beating down on the heads and the newspapers that covered them. Detachments of troops rumbled up the side streets in trucks, telelenses were trained onto the balcony, over which a heraldic tapestry had hastily been lowered. The police lines at the Bronze Door were swamped and crowds flowed over into the Square. At 12:30 P.M. the curtains behind the balcony opened and the scarlet of cardinals could be seen moving behind the windows. Then they appeared on the balcony, and Cardinal Ottaviani read in Latin: "I announce to you a great joy. We have a Pope. His name is Giovanni-Battista. . . ."

"Montini!" the crowd roared. People congratulated and embraced each other as if from now on all would be well with the world. Then, strangely, when the Pope himself appeared, the applause was moderate. He stood there on the balcony, motioning and greeting, a tiny white figure, waving arms elegantly in a stylized way that was somehow remembered. It was as though Pius XII were waving at us from the balcony.

A Dutch bishop, fellow guest at the Casa Unitas, had been smuggled into the Vatican that morning. This very distinguished-looking, white-haired man had found a way: "I borrowed scarlet and especially those indispensable silver buckles for my shoes that stamped me sufficiently as an insider. Still, I was petrified that they would spot me as an interloper, but everybody was so excited that I was not even noticed. Anyway, I believe there were more interlopers than insiders." He grinned. "And after the unlocking of the Conclave, there was such a rush around the new Pope that the poor man's arm was pinned behind his back and nearly broken."

Later, Cardinal Bea said that even before Paul VI appeared on the balcony, he had already said to him: "You just go on as before." And he had named Cardinal Cigognani to the same function that Pope John had given him, Secretary of State. This was a demonstration of continuity, but not of progressiveness, for Cigognani was known to be an arch-conservative.

Paul VI made a good start. He reassured the world, and he continued to reassure it when the next day, in his first radio message, he said: "The most important place in our pontificate will be occupied by the continuation of the Ecumenical Council, on which are fixed the eyes of all men of goodwill. This will be our principal work and in it we intend to spend all the energies the Lord has given us."

At the Casa Unitas the Protestant observers looked at one another apprehensively when his formulation—"We open our arms to all those who glory in the name of Christ. We call them by the sweet name of brothers. . . . They will find in Rome their Father's house."— came through our radio. Was the door that had been opened to lead to a one-way passage once again? On the basis of previous announcements of Cardinal Montini, they discounted this pessimistic interpretation of his words after a while. "We must give him a chance," they agreed.

On the day after the papal election I was on my way to the Vatican when I noticed an excited crowd near the Piazza Navona. Policemen were rerouting cars and buses. The ubiquitous gangs of tamed Roman toughs with lacquered hair were being distributed throughout the crowd by the mean, paunchy detective usually on duty in the Colonnade.

A dense mass of photographers was concentrated opposite the Spanish Pontifical College in its narrow, dark alley that is hardly a street.

Then, after the excited ritualistic confusion of gesturing and whistling officials, motor-police swung around the corner into the alley. Paul VI sat in his long Mercedes convertible, waving and bestowing his sweet-and-sour smile through the open window on his Romans.

The Mercedes described a majestic curve into the alley, its driver counting on completing it into the dark gate of the Spanish College. There it got stuck. Desperately, it tried to reverse a few times, like a terrier trying to pull its head out of a too-small rabbit hole.

The crowd broke through the police lines, the photographers went berserk and climbed onto the Mercedes. Colonel Angelini of the *gendarmería Pontifica* looked as if he were going to weep; he was pushing with both hands against the human flood. Then, suddenly, the top of the convertible raised itself and the slim white figure of the Pope rose with it like a jack-in-the-box. He was standing in his car and was laughing heartily.

He then entered the College on foot amidst a roar of gaiety that approached delirium, and went to visit the old Spanish cardinal Pla y Daniel, who was lying sick in his bed.

The first audience the new pope gave to the press took place three days later. Several hundred sweating journalists were gathered at the Bronze Door. We were herded up endless stairs, through miles of hallways to the high floor where the audience was to take place. For half an hour we stood compressed like pilchards in an airless, boiling corridor, decorated by Raphael, before the doors to the audience-chamber opened.

Sweating, we clambered over benches covered with green billiard-table cloth to fight for the best spots. It was an endless wait in the hot, unventilated room. At last Cardinals Alfrink and Suenens came in through a side door and talked to acquaintances. When Pope Paul finally arrived and sat on his throne he too looked dispirited and bothered by the heat. He started to read his prepared speech, discovered to his annoyance that the sheets were still stuck together and angrily threw the paper clip at the thin, startled Capovilla who had been Pope John's secretary. The Pope spoke about his father, who had been a journalist too. He was trying to establish some kind of rapport with his hearers. I hardly listened, but took in the lonely, ashen, preoccupied face of the man on the throne and drew. He re-

Pope Paul at his first audience for the press

mained rather immobile, and his expression did not change until at the end some of the most prominent newsmen came to kneel and kiss his ring. I only saw a worried man, on whom destiny had imposed the terrifying task of replacing the irreplaceable John XXIII.

On Coronation Day, Sunday, June 30, 1963, it was unbearably sultry. My ticket assigned me to the top of the Colonnade. It is surprisingly roomy up there among the weathered statuary. A few thousand privileged spectators sat on grandstands, overlooking St. Peter's Square. The photographers around me were having a fine time with their telelenses, but you cannot draw through a telelens.

At the end of the Colonnade was a window not washed for centuries, but through it you could look down on the *Scala Regia*. Just as I discovered it, Pope Paul on his seasickness-provoking contraption was being carried down the great staircase on the shoulders of figures in scarlet and magenta. A few minutes later he emerged from the Bronze Door, protected from the sun by a baldachin carried by sixteen bearers. The tiny figure was making his stylized, mechanical gestures and a roar rose up from the solid mass of humans, strewn like seeds over St. Peter's Piazza. In the glitter of the sun, scarlet and

...during Pope Paul's coronation...

gold, the *sedia* and its baldachin stopped for Archbishop Dante to burn the traditional strands of flax with the three times repeated ancient words: "Holy Father, thus passeth the glory of the world." *"Sic transit gloria mundi."*

Then the papal procession proceeded to the altar that yesterday was still being hammered together. On the benches for diplomats and royalty, flanking the altar, I could see, small as an insect, the Queen of the Belgians in her white mantilla.

It was impossible to draw from up there. It looked like a plateful of black caviar, this piazza. Carrying my sketchbook I began to wander around, hoping against hope to find a better spot. There were half a million necks there below, stretching up; every inch of space surrounding the ceremony was occupied. I bumped into one of my gendarme friends, splendid in his gala uniform, tricornered hat, and sword.

"Professore," he asked, "where are you going?" "I don't know," I growled, "but if I can't get closer, I may as well go home."

I continued to walk through the now deserted corridors of the Vatican. Again providential luck was to come to my rescue. Turning a corner, I found myself face to face with Tenente Martelli, nervously biting his fingernails, wondering whether to go right or left. "Get me closer by, Tenente, please," I pleaded.

He spread his hands, smiled up into my eyes: *"Professore,* please! Look down, those princesses are standing, those diplomats could not get in!" He took my sketchbook and started to leaf through it, paused amused at a drawing of gold-braided diplomats. "Oh, if I could only draw," he exclaimed. "But I must go." He started trotting, motioning me to follow him down a staircase. To the right there was a door. A Swiss guard presented arms, then held the door open. I found myself agape, a few feet from the papal throne, in the middle of a choir just starting to sing the Mass. "Okay now?" Martelli asked, spreading his palms again. I started to walk around a bit.

In the portico of St. Peter's, chamberlains were sitting in corners, gossiping and glad to be out of the still-burning sun, Noble Guards were standing at attention with their banner, waiting for a sign to go "on-stage." A horse-faced abbess was doggedly attempting to buttonhole a rotund archbishop. He tried desperately to dodge her. An aristocratic couple, too late to find seats, were walking up and down, quarreling in disgruntled dignity.

I walked out again, hiding amidst the choir of the Lateran University, which was singing the responses to the Mass. On the bars of the bronze gates of the Basilica young priests were hanging by hands and feet like monkeys, watching the scene below. When the Pope climbed to his throne, I stood on my little stool and drew. I drew the Pope, the cardinals, the choir, the Colonnade and even the TV cameras. Dusk was slowly falling. As if drawing balanced on that little stool were not difficult enough, the singers around me pushed and shoved to see what I was doing, until I fell over, stool and all. "Damned idiots," I growled, pointing toward the Pope, "you are here to look at *him,* not at me." They obviously understood English!

Pope Paul sat through the ceremony in utter self-collectedness. His face was solemn, its expression completely withdrawn, as if he were the passive, invulnerable victim of a sacrifice. The moment Cardinal Ottaviani placed the modern silver tiara, given by the workers of Milan, on his head his face disappeared behind the Cardinal's sleeve.

It was dark now, a deep Prussian blue darkness with mauve streaks under the arc lights. The triumphant spectacle was ebbing. Pope Paul gave his long coronation address in Latin, Italian, and French, and followed it by short homilies in six other languages.

What we waited for in the address came: The Pope promised a continued dialogue with non-Catholic Christians and, very explicitly, also with the secular world.

The show was over. The great of this world were pushing their way to their cars, meanwhile bowing, curtseying, or giving military salutes, exchanging perfunctory smiles and pleasantries, swinging top hats in gallant arcs, holding kepis elegantly before bellies.

As if a dam had collapsed, the human lake of St. Peter's Piazza spilled into the Via della Conciliazione.

It had been a Cecil B. De Mille splurge on a multimillion-dollar budget. Modern states may have abandoned their ritualistic borrowings from the Church; the Church still uses the imperial, royal, and feudal props of its history.

"What is the Papacy but the ghost of the Roman Empire sitting crowned on the grave thereof?" Hobbes asked.

It is more, as we had seen in these last few years.

Second Session

To the artist's eye the spectacle had been a delight. This whirl of flowing robes and togas, these helmets and damascened breastplates, these busbies, silver scepters and maces, crowns and jewel-encrusted crosses, this *sedia gestatoria,* wafted by the huge ostrich feathers of the *flabella,* bobbing through incredible crowds. Imagine the entire ritual performed in black and charcoal-gray clergymen suits with fedoras and clerical collars!

It is far too easy to scoff at all this pomp, this cinematographic panoply of past triumphs, for it symbolizes, however incompletely, a continuity with an unbroken history receding into the deep past, the very continuity of Western civilization from its inception. At the same time it shows up a deficiency of the Church as a worldwide, universal Church, for it is too exclusively tied to that especially Western past. Fragments of all its historic periods, from Roman robes through medieval habits, Renaissance armor, Napoleonic tunics, to the television booths on the Colonnade, are integrated in an overpowering demonstration of the perennial vitality of a structure that has known how to survive all catastrophes of history. Granted that this spectacle has little to do with man's spiritual life and his search, granted even that it is in ludicrous contradiction to the simplicity of the Gospels, still, might it perhaps be precisely this mythical camouflage, this façade of fiction, this historical theatricality that gives the Church a stability of form behind which the overdue reforms and renewals can safely be prepared? Could it be that

behind this reassuringly traditional décor of miters, crosiers, and gilded paraphernalia, the new spirit can safely grow strong?

When I arrived once more in Rome it was toward the middle of the Council's second session. The weather was as fresh and bril-

. . . the buses arrive again

liantly sunny as it would remain until the end in early December; a
cool sunshine clothed the buzzing old city in delicate pinkish-gray

and soft ochre. But the air of festivity that had conquered the continuous rain last autumn had gone.

The radiance on the faces of the *periti* and the observers had dulled. The worry, fatigue, and doubt of a workaday world had replaced the euphoria of the Joannine Council days.

The Council had become a fixture of contemporary life, a marginal fixture even in Rome itself, where the people took it for granted, hardly aware of its existence.

In the Augustinian Seminary, close to the Vatican, I was told, students were not to show any knowledge that a Council was going on. In other seminaries the writings of the new theologians were forbidden and could only be read in secret, as if they were pornography. Pope John, who had raised such hope, such confidence in the future of his Church and of man, was dead. His successor was still a riddle, a reserved, rather silent and sad-looking man, whose utterances were all right so far as they went, but still—

"If that Council just got on a bit faster, I might yet die a Catholic," Heinrich von Brentano, the former German foreign minister, had said to a journalist I met in the plane. But he and many others would die without that consolation.

It did not look as if the Council was going to establish any speed records. Pope Paul had appointed four moderators to streamline the discussions during the second session. Three of these cardinals were known for their energy and progressive tendencies: the saintly Lercaro of Bologna; the forceful dynamo, Doepfner of Munich; the intellectual, diplomatic Suenens of Belgium; and, as a concession to the Curia, everyone surmised, Cardinal Agagianian. But something or somebody had slowed down even the moderators, who were known to be far from unanimous. The dramatic clashes between "progressives" and "reactionaries" of the first session were absent. Before long the laborious daily congregations had tired out the Council Fathers, many of them quite old. It also seemed as if the great expectations of those outside St. Peter's had died: the people had seen their bishops come home to their dioceses, yet everything went on as before. No reforms had taken place, and the faithful were being told that Rome was not built in a day, nor could it be expected to change in a day.

People outside the Church are apt to make stricter demands on it than those inside. This has perhaps become even more so since John

XXIII. It is as if a deep nostalgia makes many of us long to see the Church as the ultimate moral lighthouse, even though, paradoxically, we reject its theological premises and its disciplines. Was it not revealing that as soon as Pope John stepped out of the prison of papal protocol and showed himself as a moral force, he was surrounded by the "unbelievers" and adored by them? All that was needed was for an old man to stop condemning and anathematizing and to speak convincingly in the spirit of love: the nations of the world turned their eyes toward him, full of hope and childlike confidence. Pope John's spirit, his openness, and social responsibility compensated for the malaise and disappointment that Pius XII's ambiguous, diplomatic approach had caused, perhaps less to Catholics, to whom, after all, he was their Pope, than to those countless others who demanded a moral and spiritual example on St. Peter's throne, as if saying: "If the Pope does not act as a Christian, who will?"

Pope John had been this example made flesh. His Ecumenical Council, although a great congress of the Church, by the Church, and for the Church, became a focus of hope for all men.

But the expectations and the hope raised at the beginning of the Council had certainly not yet been fulfilled. An *aggiornamento* had not yet been achieved. The great heart of Pope John had stopped and it had left us *Pacem in Terris,* but in the Council itself the great problems of war, hunger, population explosions had not even been brushed. Now, with half the second session gone, there seemed to be no chance of these problems even being placed on the agenda. Vociferous reactionaries, such as Cardinal Ruffini of Palermo, still made pronouncements that assumed the Catholic laity to be foolish juveniles devoid of even a grain of spirituality, and that insulted Protestants and Jews gratuitously. He and his kind were still beating the drum of blind obedience.

Obedience! Many inside the Church wanted to know more precisely and in clearer language to what they were supposed to be obedient. The uprooted, collectivized, mechanized man of the 1960's, far removed from the Church, had looked hopefully to the Council for nourishment, but the Council had let him continue to starve. It had not yet pronounced itself on ecumenism, on religious liberty, on the questions of war and conscientious objection in an

[151]

Archbishop Roberts, S.J.

era of total nuclear menace, on the position of the Church toward the Jews and the other non-Christian world religions. On the contrary, Archbishop Thomas Roberts, S.J.—the remarkable ex-Archbishop of Bombay who had resigned in order to make it possible for the present Cardinal Gracias, an Indian, to take his place—had been severely rebuked for daring to propose ever since 1959 a preconciliar commission to confront Christian morality with recent developments in science, medicine, military strategy, and international law. He felt that such a study for peace, supported by the prestige of the Holy See and the Council, would have been a great contribution to both the Church and the world.

Could such bold steps be seriously expected when in the field of ecumenism it had not yet become possible to refer to the non-Catholic Protestant churches as anything but "religious communities"—after all, they do call themselves churches—and when these "communities" as such had not yet been drawn into the dialogue?

The German Lutheran observer, Professor Edmund Schlink, remarked that these very "communities" had not been mentioned as such in the schema on the Church; it limited itself to speaking of non-Catholics only as individuals, thus confirming the doubt often discussed among Protestant observers privately, the doubt as to whether there really is a new spirit abroad or whether only a more polite form of speech has been adopted, in which one no longer speaks of "heretics" but of "separated brethren" and meanwhile professes a pseudo-ecumenism that intends "the absorption of divided Christians by one of the existing churches, namely, the Roman Church, instead of the communion of the divided churches."

Such was the atmosphere of Rome in mid-second session. Even the Ladies of Bethany with their indomitable courage and optimism appeared to be worried. My neighbors at the Casa Unitas this time were the American Quaker observer, Professor Douglas Steere of Haverford College, and Pasteur Hébert Roux, delegate of the Reformed World Alliance. Pasteur Roux, the most important French Protestant at the Council aside from Oscar Cullmann, is tall, angular, and outspoken. He said in his public utterances that the dialogue between Protestants and the Catholic Church placed on his coreligionists the obligation to find their own unity first and that they could take the self-examination to which the Church was subjecting itself as a lesson to be followed. Yet while I was drawing him he said: "However much they reform, unless they succeed in getting rid of their juridical and legalistic obsessions, the Council will not amount to much."

Another neighbor was the liberal Dutch Protestant observer, Professor Van Holk of Leyden University. In the small chapel of Casa Unitas, a place of noble simplicity, we non-Catholics occasionally attended Sunday Mass. On my first Sunday we sat in front of the liturgical altar, the ten chairs occupied about equally by Catholics and non-Catholics. Bishop Van Cauwelaert, son of an aristocratic Flemish family, who had stayed at his post in the Congo during all its recent upheavals, is still young. His face, thin and pale with a wisp of blond goatee, seemed copied from one of the great Van Dyck portraits. He stood there, welcoming his improvised congregation with a warmly courteous gesture and a "Be welcome at this table, my friends."

Bishop Van Cauwelaert celebrated Mass in the quiet white chapel with great concentration and fervor. We followed in our missals. After the *Ite missa est* he asked Professor Van Holk to say a few words. Moved, timid, the Dutchman got up, pulled down his sweater, fumbled a bit with his hands, which he then folded in front of him, and said: "We share with you your anguish that the Council may yet pave the way to our closer union. We share with you the conviction that only a theology of love can bring this reunion closer."

In the little chapel of Unitas we were far from the polemics of the newspapers and the disputes between "conservatives" and "progressives." Here, the spirit of John XXIII was very much alive.

Meanwhile, in St. Peter's, an endless debate for and against the collegiality of the bishops was continuing. After two weeks of "study" (in fact, it was a fierce, unabated struggle behind the scenes—there was even a rumored papal intervention), five points were to be voted upon. On October 30, 1963 an orientation vote was taken on these points. They were accepted by the overwhelming majority of bishops. The five questions defined the principles of the collegiality of the bishops. They were:

1. Is the bishop's consecration the highest degree of the sacrament of orders?
2. Is a duly consecrated bishop, consecrated in the communion of bishops and of the Pope, who is their head, a member of the College of Bishops?
3. Is the College of Bishops the successor of the College of Apostles and does it enjoy full and sovereign authority over the whole Church together with the Pope, and never without him as head, his primacy over all pastors and faithful remaining intact?
4. Does this power belong to the College of Bishops by divine right?
5. Do you agree to have the schema state that it is considered opportune to found the diaconate as a distinct, permanent degree of the ministry according to its usefulness to the Church as determined by region?

This vote meant that again a page had been turned in the history of the Church, and that the Council of Pope John had completed the disastrously interrupted work of Vatican I, which in 1870 had ruled in its decree *Pastor Aeternus* that the Pope had the sole right to govern and to administer the entire Church. It took nearly a hundred years to add: This may be so, but the College of Bishops has an analogous function for the whole Church: a bishop is not merely a branch manager for the central authority in Rome, but through his membership in the College he becomes more autonomous in his own diocese and participates in the government of other dioceses. Pope and College become complementary sovereignties over the Church, but since the Pope is the head of the College, these sovereignties cannot be opposed to each other.

The expression "divine right" shocked at first. It was too reminiscent of the pretensions of monarchs. During the luncheons at the Casa Unitas, with the Ladies of Bethany pouring their good wine for Council Fathers and theologians, I heard the problem discussed constantly and became not only familiar with such problems as that of "divine right" but also involved in them. That particular expression, indeed, serves to emphasize the point that the universal authority of the College of Bishops is considered to be not a human invention but one established by the will or wish of Christ Himself; that it is not a matter of repealable ecclesiastical law but an unchangeable verity.

I learned a great deal while drawing these men in animated conversation, such theologians as Gregory Baum, the Augustinian advisor to the Bishop of Toronto and consultant to the Secretariat for the Promotion of Christian Unity; the famous Austrian Karl Rahner, S.J.; such liberal bishops as Elchinger and de Provenchères, the forceful American bishop, John Wright of Pittsburgh; the courageous, anti-apartheid Archbishop Hurley of Durban, and Mon-

Bishop Elchinger
of Strasbourg

Professor Karl Rahner, S.J.

signor Willebrands, who is Cardinal Bea's first assistant. When, after the straw vote of October 30 and the subsequent frontal attack by Cardinal Frings on Cardinal Ottaviani, the frail, nearly blind German cardinal visited the Casa Unitas, the euphoria of the first session seemed to have been reborn.

"After a century, then," as Monsignor Edelby, patriarchal Vicar to Maximos IV * expressed it, "a morbid obsession with the primacy of the Pope" had come to an end. Cardinal Suenens of Belgium declared: "The indication of the massive vote in favor of collegiality and of the diaconate will not only facilitate the work of the doctrinal commission, but will save months and months of work. The Commission will know how to orient itself and avoid to prepare texts, for which there is no two-thirds majority. From now on the basic orientation of the Council is clear."

No wonder that violent reactions emanated from the Curia, which as the Court of the Bishop of Rome had identified itself with the primacy.

Since the foundation of the Supreme Congregation of the Holy Office in 1542 by Pope Paul III, it, and with it the Curia, had ruled supreme. Since 1870, moreover, it had spoken as if speaking for the Pope, had acted as a supreme authority—universal, direct, and perpetual—over the whole Church, instead of acting in a consultative and executive role. It had shown the power to overrule the will of

* Monsignor Edelby resigned in protest when Patriarch Maximos accepted the Cardinalcy.

the Pope, and certainly that of the bishops, however consecrated as successors of the Apostles they may be, both individually and collectively. The Curia was now ready to defend these privileges bitterly. Cardinal Ottaviani made it clear that collegiality was not yet a foregone conclusion:

October 30 was nothing but an opinion vote, he maintained, and continued: "Only the Theological Commission [of which Ottaviani is Chairman] can judge." His allies rallied around him promptly; Cardinals Browne and Ruffini, Monsignors Carli and Florit filled the air with their sinister *caveamus, caveamus* ("careful, careful"). But men like Bishop Mendes Arcéo, bold restorer of the Cathedral of Cuernavaca, declared: "We are not here to repeat Vatican I, but to complete it and to take care of the well-being of souls." And: "This well-being requires collegiality." Cardinal Doepfner denounced the curial machinations bitterly: "It might be suspected," he said, "that the last few days the Holy Spirit has been absent from this *aula*. The vote had been decided by the moderators, competent organ for the direction of the Council. And the formula 'College of Bishops' was

Cardinals Browne and Ruffini in a discussion

lifted from the text of the draft already approved by the Theological Commission."

Of course, the principle of collegiality had not yet been confirmed in an official decree, and it was still to be tested whether the Theological Commission under its intransigent chairman is the servant or the judge of the Council.

Cardinal Frings of Cologne asserted: "The Holy Office must be reformed. The old Inquisition causes torment in the souls and scandal in the world." And he concluded: "Nobody should ever any more be judged and condemned without even a hearing, without knowledge of what he is accused of, without the possibility of correcting what he is accused of."

It will be far from easy to reform the Holy Office. Although nominally the Pope is its prefect, or chairman, its Secretary (now Cardinal Ottaviani) is the acting chief. Since it has worldwide jurisdiction over all Catholics in matters of faith and morals, it wields power over all the other "congregations," or ministries. To make its hold on the other ministries more complete, the heads of the most crucial ministries (the Secretariat of State, the congregation that nominates bishops, the congregation that regulates studies, the one that deals with the discipline of secular priests and the laity) are members of the Supreme Congregation of the Holy Office, as are nearly all the prelates in charge of Vatican finances.

Patriarch Maximos IV spoke scathingly of the proposed smallish and timid reforms which would let some bishops be delegated to the Roman congregations: "It is an error to say that the Pope is the head of the Church; the Church has only one head, Christ." He also said: "The power of the Episcopal College in no way destroys the primacy of the Pope, but the bishops are rulers in their own dioceses, which is clear from the development of the Oriental Church since apostolic times," and "The dogma of the primacy of the Roman pontiff has led to abusive interpretations which have disfigured it."

According to the prominent Dutch theologian, Professor Haarsma: "The Curia has proven conclusively in connection with the October 30 vote that it is in great need of reform, not just in secondary details, but in an entirely new definition of its very task. The theological basis for this reform has been prepared by the adoption of collegiality by the Council. The Curia has proven that it intends to eclipse this rediscovered realization of the episcopal

LEFT:
Cardinal Frings

BELOW:
Cardinal Doepfner

function. While assisting the Pope in the exercise of his function as Head of the College of Bishops and Patriarch of the West, it limits and cramps the bishops in the exercise of their duties by usurping so many of their functions that bishops have become representatives of the central Roman authority rather than autonomous shepherds. The Curia has become more of a wall between bishops and Pope than an instrument of communication. It now has to become a servant and purely an executive instrument of the Pope."

Had not Pope Paul himself said substantially the same on September 21?

The debate on collegiality became a sign that a process of clarification was at work in which the bishops expressed their conviction that they did not derive their mission from a papal, or rather a curial, appointment, but that it came from an infinitely higher source—as expressed here, "through their consecration, directly from Christ." Couldn't it be that if this process continued, it would embrace the priesthood, and ultimately the laity, in a greater realization of mutual responsibility and love, in a declaration of interdependence, another metaphor for the Mystical Body? Was this perhaps why the debate on collegiality was deemed worth the attention of a world, faced with the not inconsiderable practical problems of sheer survival? And was it this that the Curia feared most?

In those days I was drawing Abbot Christopher Butler of Downside, Superior General of the English Congregation of the Order of St. Benedict. Meeting him, there was an immediate feeling of contact. The abbot is young-looking and slim. He lives in the Abbey of San Anselmo, high on the Aventine Hill. I had clambered up from the Tiber and was still out of breath when I asked for him. The bald German brother *portiere* looked at me suspiciously.

A pipe-smoking Englishman with a twinkle in his eye rescued me: "Ready to pose!" cried the Abbot, and ran a little in front of me up the stone staircase to his room. "I hope I'll do you justice," I said as the Abbot stood in the middle of a room full of books—on shelves, chairs, and floor—filling his pipe. "Help yourself," said the Abbot, shoving the tobacco at me, "and don't do me justice, but mercy!"

A former Anglican priest, he had just missed becoming the Archbishop of Westminster and hence almost certainly a cardinal. Too outspoken? Too liberal? He was obviously one of the very best, and the very best in this Church of Rome are the most delightful, humane, and wise men of the world and men of the spirit. I found myself, before I knew it, talking about the allergy so many of us contemporary men have against theological phraseology, and about what seemed to me, as a non-Catholic layman, the most demanding task of those who guard our spiritual heritage: to circumvent that allergy, to stop estranging exactly those who are most preoccupied with the meaning of their lives. How to extend the ecumenical thought to those who are outside the organized religions? Because amongst those numberless unaffiliated people are to be found thousands whose ultimate concern is with the meaning of existence, who are committed to a search for this meaning as the goal toward which all other meanings point. Precisely there one should look for and

*Abbot
Christopher Butler
of Downside*

channel the greatest reservoir of spiritual or religious energy in our time. There is enough of this energy to transform and transcend the materialism and the inertia that pervades the official culture on both sides of the Iron Curtain. The really important demarcation line today is not so much between Catholics and Protestants, but between materialism and the inertia that pervade the official culture on both those who believe that we are here to discover the ultimate meaning of our human lives and those who trust in redemption by the gadget, by next year's model car, freezer, pill or rocket.

The abbot sat there listening, smoking his pipe, which was sticking up hiding the tip of his nose, his hands poised on his typewriter.

"I am sorry, Father Abbot," I apologized. "I came here to draw, not to disturb you. I don't know what emboldened me to sound off in this tirade, or shall we say 'intervention'?"

"There are many in the Church," he said, "who see it as a set of propositions from which you can derive an infinite number of further propositions. Of course, they do not see that if you hold us to this view, we do not need Grace or a Holy Spirit at all!" As he continued, I grew fonder of him and I understood why I had felt compelled to talk.

"Did you see that cartoon in *The New Yorker*," he asked, "of the computer that delivers answers to a set of questions fed to it? One scientist, who is standing by it, is looking at the answer in bafflement. 'What does it say?' asks the other. 'It says, *"Cogito, ergo sum!"* ' "

"But how can you draw if I don't keep quiet?" he said, taking the blame for what I had started. He relit my pipe and then his own and started to type away.

He was delighted with the drawing: "It will give my colleagues a lot of fun, because they are always ribbing me about my pipe."

He gave me a book on the First Vatican Council by his namesake Dom Cuthbert Butler, inscribed "To console you for the Second Session." I treasure this nearly as much as the book Cardinal Bea gave me, especially after what happened a few days later, when the Auxiliary Bishop of Sidney complained in the Council: "There are some here who return constantly to the forgiveness to be asked by the Catholic Church. If there are those who make mistakes, let them look for a good confessor instead of talking constantly about this matter." Dom Butler jumped to the microphone and replied: "We cannot hide in the confessional and take a place amongst the Pharisees, leaving to the others the place of the Publicans. Recognition and forgiveness of faults are the essence of ecumenism. I don't know if the echoes of the historical events of the Reformation have ever penetrated as far as Australia. But here these faults are admitted by historians. The Council must join the Pope in the asking of forgiveness."

I simply *had* to get into St. Peter's during an everyday session. I had not yet succeeeded. One day I had driven throughout Rome with a busload of American bishops. One of them, a very important young American prelate, had invited me to join them. The bishops behind me were discussing a good restaurant they had just discovered: "They give you a real good American steak, an inch thick, and a salad with French fries for about three dollars." They might have been Rotarians.

It all went well at first. My protector put his magenta arm around my shoulders as we alighted on the Square, and together we climbed the steps of St. Peter's. But hardly had we entered the Basilica when I felt a tap on my shoulder, and all the self-confidence of my bishop was of no avail.

A very urbane and charming Brazilian monsignor, Jerome Nabuco, an expert at the Council, assured me that he could easily manage it. To make quite sure, I gave him a copy of the letter of Archbishop Primo Principi to Cardinal Larraona, in which I was given permission to draw in the Basilica during the *sede vacante*. Monsignor Nabuco, who looked the perfect diplomat—indeed, his father and brother had each served as Brazilian ambassadors to Washington—was going to negotiate my presence at Council meetings with Archbishop Pericle Felici, Secretary-General of the Council, usually referred to as Uncle Pericle, whether because of his stratagems or his joviality I never found out. I had often looked closely at Felici—I had drawn him without being observed—and I felt quite sure that despite all his hereditary diplomacy my kind Monsignor would fail in his mission. I had seen the stocky little archbishop bounce all over the Basilica. I had seen his sly, good-humored but cautious smile, a smile that was just a bit too permanent. I had drawn that ecclesiastical prizefighter's face, and I knew the intervention could not possibly be successful.

The Archbishop had no weakness for artists; he suggested that "this fellow could perfectly well draw from the official photographs." Monsignor Nabuco was genuinely embarrassed and sad. He had done his best. To me, it meant a retreat and long meditation at the espresso bar on the Via della Conciliazione. I blamed myself for my diplomatically inept approach. Why even mention my wish to draw? Somehow one always falls again into the trap of believing that being an artist is really respectable among the serious people of this world. I would try another way.

I found it. It was complicated, and I do not want to disclose it and to cause to anybody the smiling Archbishop's animosity, which must be very unpleasant indeed. This unpleasantness was demonstrated when on November 25, 1963 the muscular prelate fought the German bishop Reuss physically on the steps of St. Peter's in order to grab a bundle of statements against the schema *De Instrumentis Communicationis* that were being distributed. He had also called on the Vatican police to help him confiscate the leaflets that bishops and priests were handing out to their own colleagues, as precedent had given them every right to do. All I can say is that I did succeed in drawing the Council.

One of the outspoken critics of the Curia was Archbishop Eugene d'Souza from Bhopal, India. I had met him at an ecclesiastical cocktail party and I liked his intelligent, intense, young Indian face. He had said in the Council that the Roman Curia should be subjected to profound reform; he spoke on that same, memorable day when Cardinal Frings had disapproved severely of the methods adopted by the Holy Office. He called attention to a schema text that read: "The Congregations of the Roman Curia fulfill their office in the name and by the authority of the Supreme Pontiff." He insisted that this was too vague a statement, and that "unless the power of the Curia is precisely defined, the state of affairs in the Church will revert to what it was before the Council, at least after a few years." He also scathingly opposed the forces that had maintained that the votes cast on October 30 on the five basic points were invalid. "I adjure you, Venerable Brothers, not to reduce these matters to a

Moderator's table

juridical aspect. What interests us most is the salvation of souls, which is the supreme law." He also spoke in favor of decentralization and reform of canon law, adapting it to various cultural contexts. He did not believe "that a few bishops from around the world, scattered among the various sacred congregations, could have any real influence as consultants if 2,200 bishops gathered together in Council have the greatest difficulty in not succumbing to certain pressures." As one of his desiderata he offered this: "On the one hand, the power of the Curia should be limited, and on the other hand the bishops might be granted all the faculties which belong to them by common and divine law for the exercise of their office. We are not children!" he exclaimed. Another one of Bishop d'Souza's utterances became somewhat of a proverb: "I do not fear Peter but Peter's secretaries, who with the stroke of a pen *non expedit* can bury projects which our bishops' conferences have cultivated for years."

The energetic archbishop was living at the Nordland Hotel, a new but ramshackle place in a no-man's-land of new houses and broken lots of ground. It was early afternoon, and bishops were sitting in the drab hotel lounge in shirt sleeves and suspenders studying their schemata. Archbishop d'Souza was talking into the lobby phone, a big pipe between his teeth. He spoke Indian-Oxford-English with high-piping notes and little waterfalls of vowels. He took me to his small, mean bedroom overlooking the no-man's-land. A brand-new electric shaver was lying on the chair I had to clear. "How shall I pose?" the Archbishop asked, sucking his pipe. "Why don't you read, Your Grace?" "Fine," he said, displaying his improbably beautiful teeth. "I'll read my breviary." He opened it, and continued smiling broadly. I started to scribble. The Archbishop kept smiling, his beautiful, regular front teeth indecently bare. "Okay?" he asked, maintaining the grin. What could I do? I became increasingly irritable as the smile persisted. Could I say, "Wipe it off, Your Grace" or "Is your breviary that funny?" What does protocol require when an archbishop insists on reading his breviary with a Valentino smile fixed on his face? He would have to get tired in the long run. I pretended to scribble and was sure I could outlast him. After a good quarter of an hour of indefatigable smiling, he had finished with his breviary. He still smiled unflinchingly.

"What do you think of the orientation vote, Your Grace?" I asked.

"Do you think it will be nullified?" "Oh, no, it won't," he exclaimed, looking angry suddenly. "It would be an act of derision of the Council," he said, quoting himself, "to say that there is no obligation to take into consideration the views of eighty-five per cent of the Council Fathers." Archbishop d'Souza continued his monologue, became more and more intense and serious, and proved to be a good model after all.

During the first session, after I had drawn Patriarch Stephanos Sidarous of Alexandria, I had promised to bring him a photostat of the drawing he liked. I called him and he was very pleased that I had not forgotten. "Why don't you come to Salvator Mundi tomorrow?" he said. "All seven of us patriarchs will be there."

Salvator Mundi is Rome's most luxurious hospital. It was built high above the city and overlooks it proudly from its hilltop. During the Council a number of high dignitaries were housed there. A pale American nun with a Rolleiflex was pacing up and down, waiting for Their Beatitudes to appear in the airport-modern hall. The patriarchs were late for lunch. A very fat man paid the cashier, then emerged with his suitcase into the sunlight and waited for a taxi. I stood with him and watched limousines that brought bishops and priests. The nun with the camera kept on pacing; she was whistling softly to herself.

There was a flurry behind me in the lobby. The pale nun was hopping around, smiling efficiently, taking pictures, first snapping Patriarch Pierre-Paul Méouchi, the tallest. Patriarchs Batanian and Maximos came last, joking and posing. I started to draw. Cardinal Koenig seemed to belong to the party. "Aren't you the drawing American?" he asked in good English. "Someone told me you wanted to draw me." We made an appointment in a hurry: I was now catching patriarchs! Monsignor Edelby, on the heels of Patriarch Maximos, recognized me: "You drew His Beatitude last year, didn't you? I saw your drawing somewhere." He said something in Arabic to Maximos: "You made me look *trop sévère*," the old man said. "You *looked* very severe last session, Your Beatitude," I answered, "but I'd love to do you again."

Maximos IV Sayegh sat down in the lounge against a background of cheap African souvenirs, left by some grateful bishop. The sun-

Patriarch
Maximos IV Sayegh

light made the white hair of his mane and beard shine like angel hair on a Christmas tree. This was the proud man who had stirred the Council, who had refused to walk in the opening procession because he felt that as Patriarch of Antioch he should have preceded those newcomers, the cardinals, and who spoke French instead of Latin. Patriarch Maximos looked and acted the patriarch.

As I arranged my sketchbook and started to draw, Maximos' eyes narrowed and he gave me a wide, wise smile. "Cheese," he said, "cheese, *comme on dit en Amérique!*"

"He is so wonderful," Monsignor Edelby said, after the patriarch had withdrawn for a nap. "At eighty-five getting up at four in the morning to put the last touches on his interventions, and he thinks of every detail. He is a very great man."

"Was he much affected by Pope John's death?" I asked.

"Terribly. *Il l'a tellement aimé!* And for so many years. I was in Russia when Pope John died. And there I got a cable: 'Meet me in Rome.' He already had flown to Rome; this eighty-five-year-old man, to pay his respects to his friend. He did not go anywhere and did not want to be photographed. 'I am not here to be photographed,' he said, 'I am here to take leave of my friend Roncalli.' "

Many see in Maximos IV one of the dominating personalities of the second session, who brought the notion of unity in diversity graphically to the attention of the Latin Council Fathers. During the entire second session the "Orientals" had stressed the theme of collegiality, advocated a less formalistic theology, and discussed the problem of common participation by Catholics and Orthodox in the sacraments, thus clearing the way for a greater understanding, which could lead to reunion with the Orthodox churches. It was Maximos who stressed that the Eastern-rite Catholics can show the Orthodox that union with Rome is possible without loss of their Eastern identity. In so far as unification of canonical codes would tend to favor the Latin canon law, Maximos said that "it would be disastrous to show the Orthodox that the discipline which awaits them on the day of reunion would be a Latin discipline."

I hadn't seen much of Father Eugene Hoade, my great impresario of the first session. But at last I caught him in his "shop," the first confessional on the left in St. John Lateran. He had aged considerably and did not look very well, having suffered a heart attack earlier in the year. He did not walk so cocksurely now in his soiled brown habit.

"No coffee for me any more, old boy," Father Hoade said, "but I'll have a cognac with you. No more cigarettes, either," he growled, "the old ticker is not so good. Well, whom have you drawn up till now?" He was impressed with my list of models. "Have you drawn young Conway yet?"

"Sounds Irish to me, Father Eugene. I thought you specialized in Orientals. Who is he?"

"The Most Reverend Archbishop Conway of Armagh, Primate of All Ireland. He'll be a cardinal in a couple of months, so you'd better draw him."

"I'll thank you for a good look at your new primate, Father," I said, "and I hope he's as good to draw as that fine old man D'Alton."

My appointment was at four at the Irish College, a humorless nineteenth-century building in the rear of a good front yard with crisscross paths. How the special atmosphere was transplanted I don't know, but here in the middle of Rome I was reminded of boarding-houses in Edinburgh and Dublin. It did not smell of cabbage, neither was there a slovenly landlady; still, the atmosphere was there. The waiting room had been "done over." It had been papered with silk-patterned wallpaper over an uneven wall. The double doors were painted a too-flaming knotty oak. In the center of the square room stood a marble table with over-ornamented legs. Four matching chairs with lusciously curlicued backs were arranged around it. The unavoidable Louis XV console, holding an inexpressive head of Christ in white marble, was standing next to a window. To make the atmosphere even more Scotch-Irish, it started to drizzle out on the front lawn.

It was a long wait. I paced around the room on the polished marble-tiled floor and heard Irish voices argue outside. When at last I sat down, a part of the curlicued back of my chair collapsed. I jumped up and fitted the fragment into place. It would hold until the next visitor! I went on pacing. Then the archbishop came in—a tall, heavy man, very young for an archbishop, strong as a fullback. A farmer or a farmer's son. When we went to his room, he looked at his watch.

"I am told you need only five minutes," he said, smiling.

Father Hoade had boasted again.

I started to draw, and saw a face full of energy, but narrow, systematic, rigid. After three minutes he said, matter-of-factly: "You must be about ready now; you see, I have a conference in five minutes and I still have to get my papers upstairs." "I need another minute, Your Grace," I said. Not that I did. The face did not interest me, but, wanting to save an artist's dignity, I used the extra minute to sketch a little statue standing behind him. We shook hands and in the waiting room I grabbed my coat, threw my portfolio on the table, and flung my sketches into it. A big piece of exuberant ornament fell off one of the legs. I left it on the polished marble tiles and fled, succeeding in nodding with great dignity to the janitor.

On November 21, 1963 when the debate on the schema on Ecumenism had been discussed for three days, Joseph Cardinal Ritter, Archbishop of St. Louis (Missouri) said in the Council hall that he considered "religious liberty to be a basis and prerequisite for ecumenical contacts with other Christian bodies." He added: "Without passing judgment on the validity of their orders and the celebration of the Eucharist we earnestly request that the designation 'church' not be denied them." About the declaration on religious liberty in the schema on Ecumenism, Cardinal Ritter felt that "without such a declaration, mutual confidence will be impossible and serious dialogue will be precluded." In common with some other American bishops, he elaborated on this theme, commenting on "the absolute liberty of the act of faith, the dignity of the human person and his inviolable conscience" and on "the total incompetence of the civil government in passing judgment on the Gospel of Christ and its interpretation." He also demanded "that a declaration on religious liberty should reaffirm the complete independence of the Church from any civil government in fulfilling its mission." On the chapter about the Jews, he declared that whether it belonged to this schema or not, he was "very highly pleased with it, as it clearly expressed the goals set for this Council." He called for explicit reaffirmation of the validity of orders and sacraments in the separated Oriental churches and found that the schema on Ecumenism had "at last put an end to the Counter-Reformation, with its unfortunate polemics, both theologically and historically."

In this short unambiguous statement the cardinal from St. Louis had pronounced himself in favor of all that a non-Catholic as well as many Catholics could desire from this Ecumenical Council.

I saw Francis Cardinal Spellman often, shuffling his old, heavy body into the Basilica, looking ill, preoccupied, and unhappy, the famous smile appearing only fleetingly when facing a camera. He had made himself the defender of the Curia with the Ottavianian line: "The Curia is the executive of papal power. It is chosen by the Pope. The Council has no right to criticize it." With Cardinal McIntyre, he was now in the rear guard, which, as Father Yves Congar said, "could not even put up more than an obstructive delaying action."

Cardinal Ritter, at seventy-two, looked slight and lean, with bright blue eyes and the crackled skin of a woodsman. He had forced integration in his St. Louis parochial school system in 1947, long before the Supreme Court handed down its momentous decision on integration. I looked forward to my appointment with the cardinal the next Sunday.

But on Friday evening, as I walked up the Via Veneto past the

American Embassy, I saw cars speeding through the gate. There were some onlookers as there always are when there is a reception at the Embassy. A few hundred feet farther on, a pile of newspapers was flung in front of a newsstand. I saw part of a headline: KENNEDY . . . GRAVISSIMO, and had a sinking feeling. "Another Cuban crisis" flashed through my mind. I picked up one of the papers, trying to decipher the Italian, refusing to understand. But soon I saw headlines everywhere: KENNEDY MORTE. Not more than twenty minutes could have elapsed, but now there were already hundreds of Americans, then thousands, in front of the Embassy, thousands of baffled people, asking each other, "Could this be true?" asking themselves quite irrationally: "Should I phone New York?" "Should I take a plane home?" We were all in shock. . . .

At that moment of crisis I suddenly realized, after having been a citizen of the United States for some twenty years, how much I had become an American.

"Who did it? . . . How did it happen?"

We were like children in mortal fear, standing bunched together in front of that Embassy, and mumbling. We felt ourselves to be in a foreign land, and somehow guilty of being in a foreign land, as if we could have prevented this nightmare by staying home. It was immediately assumed that the assassination was part of a plot, part of the civil rights struggle. A Negro student said, "I just hope it was not a Negro who did it." "They got him. He is a white man," a woman reassured him. "A white supremacist," somebody said. . . . a Cuban agent . . . a Communist . . . a Birchite. We stood around as if it were dangerous to leave this all-American crowd, then drifted slowly away into the empty Roman streets.

I assumed that Cardinal Ritter would cancel our appointment, but he did not. He sat in his sunny room in the very modern building of the American College, very modern but for the inevitable baroque chairs standing on the mosaic floors. My first impressions were of great simplicity, serenity, and cleanness. He looked the ideal protagonist of all that is good and loveable in America, the quite undramatic type whose image Hollywood has never exported so as to acquaint the world with it.

"I couldn't sleep last night," he said. "I should have taken a pill. It's incredible, this assassination. What a terrible warning to

Cardinal Ritter

our people! All the hatred that has been allowed to be sown over our land was bound to end in terrible, unbalanced acts like this one. What a shame! Kennedy was growing into being such an excellent President," he mused. "It is scandalous, shameful," he said again, the light-blue eyes flashing, the muscles in his old neck all at once standing out like strings. "Shameful how that civil rights legislation has been watered down and used as a political issue. After a hundred years of procrastination, couldn't we pass it proudly, unanimously, as a demonstration of the maturity of our people?"

He told me that fifteen years ago, when he was integrating his St. Louis schools, he was bombarded with bags full of hate-mail, obscene and threatening. Prominent Catholics had besieged him, slapping stacks of clippings on his desk to prove the Negro's criminality and asocial character. "I said, 'Take it away. I don't even have to look at it. This is purely a moral issue.' "

As I drew he kept on writing with a ballpoint pen, a firm, imperturbable handwriting. Then we spoke about the Council and Pope John: "He was a miracle," the Cardinal said, "a miracle sent by God. And miracles don't last; they are signs and we have to carry on with all our energy and our brains." He insisted on helping me into my coat and in accompanying me to the "temperamental" elevator, pointing out the buttons I was to press. He was not the kind of cardinal who expects you to kiss his ring.

"I am most grateful to you for posing for me," I said, "but I am even more grateful for every word you have spoken in the Council." He smiled at me, holding my hand for a minute. "Oh, excuse me, Your Eminence, I left my hat in your bedroom."

"I'll get it," he said, starting to trot back nimbly to his room. The face was strong and gentle, the carriage that of a free man, full of a dignity that does not depend on title or display. Also, it was definitely not the face of an intriguer. This man was no match for the professional schemers of this world.

Next day I attended the solemn Requiem Mass in St. Peter's. It had been planned as a Requiem Mass for the cardinals who had died during 1963, but it now became a Requiem Mass for our President. Diplomats and their ladies were present and flashbulbs were bursting like Roman candles over the Basilica. Suddenly, a doddering old cardinal with very prominent dark eyes spotted me drawing, and I saw him coming toward me, waddling across the aisle to tell me that I was desecrating the Basilica by drawing. He had a severe Parkinson tremor, poor old man, and spoke in staccato Italian. I caught something like "sacrilege." I gave him a studiously stupid smile, pretended not to understand his Italian, looked pleased, as if he were paying me ecstatic compliments, and kept bowing and saying, "Thank you, thank you, Your Eminence, you are most kind." He shrugged finally, and waddled away disconsolately, shaking his head, followed by his acolyte.

In the afternoon I drew Professor Schlink, the very Germanic Lutheran observer.

"I insist," said the Herr Professor, "on seeing the drawing after you have finished it and before publication. This is my routine with all my interviews." Protestant observers apparently can also be worried about "unserene expressions around the mouth"!

The second session of Vatican II was drawing to a close in an atmosphere of lassitude and malaise. The great promise of the Joannine Council had not been fulfilled. Even the approval of the schema

Requiem Mass for President Kennedy

on the Liturgy did little to dispel the general malaise. The subsequent unprepared, undebated approval of the schema on Mass Communications was regarded by the open-minded, as well as by non-Catholics, as a disaster, unworthy of the Council—a banal, moralistic document, narrowly clerical in spirit, lacking realization of the very basis of mass communications in the modern world, leaving the door open to state and church censorship.

It was being whispered about everywhere that the really important decisions were no longer taking place on the Council floor, where one Council Father after another made their progressive or conservative speeches, unaware that they were being used in a filibuster while a few all-powerful personalities played politico-spiritual poker behind the scenes.

The reaction of the world to the deliberations of the Council has been diagnosed acutely by Archbishop Paul Yun-Pin of Nanking. He found three main responses: a vague sympathy in those who see the Church as a worldwide structure that serves as a bulwark against communism; a mere intellectual curiosity: Could this fossil really be brought into rapport with the modern world? The most common reaction, however, was one of vast indifference in that overwhelming majority to whom liturgical and theological affairs are most uninteresting and to whom the internal reform of the Church is an internal quarrel about absurd and abstruse details. In order to influence the modern world the Council would have had to formulate a Magna Carta of a new world order, based on fundamental freedom and social justice as expressions of the dignity of the person in the Christian view and an unequivocal attitude of the Church toward war. In so far as the Council did not bring this about, the Archbishop said, mankind is right in being disappointed.

Yet at the end of this same second session my own feeling was that, in spite of the cumbersome and unfair rules of procedure under which it labored and notwithstanding the just as obvious, behind-the-scenes maneuvers that sabotaged it, something very important had taken place. The Council had revealed the fact that beneath the monolithic, static surface of the Church as it had demonstrated itself during our lifetime, suppressed but vital currents of unconventional and creative religious ideas had been at work that were now irresistibly breaking through the petrified crust. It was a deeply moving

R. Père Yves Congar

discovery in Rome to find that wherever the thinkers of these original and creative thoughts spoke there were overflow audiences of bishops, priests, and students honoring these men who had been hounded and suppressed by official Rome, some of them for decades. Wherever I heard a lecture by Küng, de Lubac, Daniélou, or John Courtney Murray, there sounded ovations that shook the foundations of curial Rome. Wherever Teilhard de Chardin was mentioned the cheers must have set the seismographs in the Holy Office rocking.

Ecumenism was here to stay. Chicanery may have prevented Professor Oscar Cullmann from speaking at the Biblical Institute, but he was heard by an overflow audience in St. Louis des Français, with five French cardinals and hundreds of bishops cheering him.

When Father Yves Congar was scheduled to speak at the Biblical Institute, the auditorium was so overfilled, with hundreds of priests packing the hallways hours before the lecture, that the program had to be transferred to the large *aula* of the Gregorian University.

The story of a man like Father Congar illustrates what the forerunners of the Council had to endure and the pressures that were used to crush them: In 1935 Father Congar wrote an article on the causes of the loss of faith in the modern world. In 1937 he founded the series *Unam Sanctam* and contributed its first volume: *Disunited Christians, Principles of a Catholic Ecumenism.* His book was found to be "dangerous," and Rome prohibited a second printing. In 1950

Congar's *True and False Reform in the Church* was immediately sold out; but additional reprintings were stopped suddenly without the author's knowledge. In 1953, when the experiment of the "worker-priests" was forbidden by Rome, Congar wrote, "Thanks to these men, the poor hear the Church. . . ." In 1954 he was forbidden to teach at Le Saulchoir Seminary. His writings were placed under Roman censorship: not that doctrinal errors could be found in them, but they were "dangerous." That same year he was banished to the Holy Land, where he wrote *The Mystery of the Temple*, which the censor kept for four years. Returned to France, and because the interdict on teaching at a seminary was still in force, he accepted an opportunity to teach at the Sorbonne. Immediately before the beginning of the term he was summoned to Rome by telegram and had to abandon all his plans. He remained completely unemployed for a year. In 1955 the new General of his order tried to employ him again at Le Saulchoir Seminary. But Rome was watching. Father Congar was sent to England. In Cambridge he was forbidden contact with his ecumenical friends until, in 1957, Archbishop Weber of Strasbourg invited him and became his defender. Pope John saw Congar's true value. He made him a consultant to the Preparatory Theological Commission. It is inexplicable what reserves of fidelity, grace, and wisdom have kept men like Congar, de Lubac, Chenu, John Courtney Murray faithful to their enlightened views and, more miraculously, to the Church.

The current of living water, then, under the frozen surface of the Church, was fed by slowly matured biblical research, profound reflections on the liturgy, and on pastoral theology in confrontation with the reality of man's condition.

This resulted in the vision of not only Christian unity but also, unavoidably, of human unity and brotherhood. What else could a deepened religious consciousness bring? Also, it would naturally aspire to wholeness, and hence have to reject systems of doublethink in which highflown theological abstractions must be tailored to fit cynical opportunism. A deepened experience of the Reality toward which all the metaphors of dogma, all the verbal accounts of revelation point inevitably produced a greater tolerance of conceptual diversity. In the middle of the twentieth century, a mutation in man's religious consciousness was taking place. Pope John felt it in his certainty that his initiative for a Council was an inspiration from the Holy Spirit.

An irresistible ground swell was changing the Church notwithstanding the Curia's bitter opposition. Attitude, emphasis, outlook, ritual, had changed after more than four hundred years of paralysis.

Forward-looking bishops, priests, and laymen had supported this elite of theologians, linguists, exegetes, ecumenists. Then during the Council the sheer number of bishops influenced by this profoundly spiritual renewal and rejuvenation had come as a shocking surprise to those to whom *Romanità* meant that massive incrustation of frozen theological theorems and juridical constructs which for centuries had remained their guarantee of invulnerable authoritarian privilege.

Could the Curia seriously be expected to surrender this absolute power, wielded uninterruptedly since the Middle Ages? It is naïve to view this Curia as a collection of malevolent old plotters. It represents the residue of a dead, feudal "status culture," but it is a residue still powerfully alive in the midst of the pluralistic society of the twentieth century. It will not, and cannot, obligingly evaporate and leave a vacuum at the center of the complex historical structure of the Church. First, new and competent institutions must be formed, which, through awareness of the social problems of the times, through sensitiveness to the spiritual plight of modern man, and through experience with non-Mediterranean mentalities, are ready to replace or rejuvenate the Curia.

For the time being, profiting from their strategic positions in the conciliar commissions and their knowledge of political chicanery, the Curia had blocked Pope John's *aggiornamento*.

Yet the 21st Ecumenical Council had taken place, and the Church would never be the same again. Pope John had died and his successor, faced with the superhuman task of replacing one who had been superhuman, had certainly not undone what John had initiated. Was it realistic to demand of this cautious intellectual statesman, formed in the world of the Vatican Foreign Office, to proceed with the intuitive audacity of the visionary prophet who had preceded him?

The Council had certainly not yet miraculously transformed the Church into that spiritual beacon longed for by all mankind; it had not even begun to solve the tragicomic family squabble within Christianity. Yet it had not been without achievements:

It had overwhelmingly approved in principle a theology of the collegiality of bishops to supplement the theology of papal infallibility and primacy. It had opted for "Peter and the *other* Apostles" as against "Peter and the Apostles." It had obtained a liturgical reform that would change the Church from within, from its heart, by the use of the vernacular in the liturgy, by involving the laity in it, by giving a greater place to the Gospels in the liturgy, by restoring the communal nature of the Church. The liturgy had been reestablished as an act of the "people of God" instead of being a spectacle for the "sheep." There is a great evolution from the triumphalist self-satisfaction that had repelled the multitudes to the self-awareness of being a "people of God," a "community of sinners."

The Council had checked, even though by a small margin only, the independent, excessive growth of Mariology by placing it within the total structure of the Church. It had reawakened an awareness in the laity of being an integral part of the Church instead of just "belonging" to it: a layman, Professor Jean Guitton, had already spoken in St. Peter's.

The Council had attempted to end the Church's identification with the rich and powerful, and had called on the Church to humble herself and to identify with the needy and downtrodden.

It had accepted ecumenism, and many had been the voices that had emphasized as its most important ingredients self-examination, soul-searching, repentance for iniquities committed, and inner renewal through return to the evangelical and patristic sources.

True, these achievements had not yet been confirmed in official decrees; true, the Council had "petered out," and the solemnly promised votes on religious liberty and on the relationship with the Jews had still been prevented by suspect and deliberate delays. The moderators could have ordered these votes; the Council could have demanded them. Yet, while applauding Cardinal Bea and Bishop De Smedt, champions of these all-important statements, the Council let the opportunity slip by. Also by omission, it let the opportunity pass to vote down the regressive schema on Mass Communications.

Notwithstanding the Council's positive achievements, however, there remains the disturbing fact, not to be overlooked, that in this "open Council" the will of a clear majority has been effectively squashed, up to this point, whenever hidden forces have deemed it necessary. It can also not be overlooked that the general approval of ecumenism in the abstract does not signify a consensus as to its precise meaning. Opportunistic political considerations had most probably blocked the votes on religious liberty and the Jews.

Yet there was reason to hope that the old stereotype of the static Catholic Church had weakened in the hearts of participants and observers alike. The ground had been prepared; good seed had been sown. There would be another nine months of dangerous gestation. Would there be drought or rain; would there be harvest or famine and a disaster that would encompass infinitely more than the Catholic Church alone? After John XXIII how could the Church still dare to speak of "dialogue" without freedom? How could it still function in the pluralistic world with its resurgence of Asian, African, and Middle-Eastern cultures without decentralization? How could the universal message of the Church be transmitted except by diversification? Cultural as well as spiritual imperialism had clearly had its day. How could a church that regards its laymen as "belonging" to it, instead of recognizing their freedom of conscience to choose it, their spiritual potential to embody it, avoid being increasingly regarded as a hierarchical machine?

The laity could no longer be expected to see themselves as third-rate citizenry, the passive objects of the ministrations of the hierarchy, as if they were still illiterate, as at the time of the Council of Trent, as if they had not yet shaken off the tyranny of kings, nobles, and colonial powers.

"For four hundred years the faithful have been waiting for a positive conciliar statement on the place, dignity, and vocation of the layman," Bishop John Wright of Pittsburgh had declared in the Council, contradicting Cardinal Ernesto Ruffini, who had expressed his fear that "the laity feels it has a juridical right to share in the mission of the Church" and that "this could lead to a weakening of the position of the hierarchy. . . ."

Could the Church still lay claim to Christianity after Auschwitz and after "I am Joseph, your brother," while silently tolerating the semiofficial anti-Semitism that has continued to poison Christian education for millennia? Could it avoid the problems of human relations in general, those of East to West, of Europe to America, of Catholics to non-Catholics, of racism in South Africa and in the United States? Could it afford the Curia's seeming unawareness of the very real problems of the human race: population explosion and birth control, peace and atomic war, coexistence with Russia and China, the unity of Europe, scientific developments in physics, genetics, psychology, and their inevitable results in new techniques and philosophies?

In our age of space exploration could absolute power remain in the hands of a group which, notwithstanding all divine pretensions, has demonstrated to the world its all too human intellectual, historical, sociological, and ethical deficiencies?

In this changed world, reforms are being forced upward through the pyramid of power and may blow off its lid. *"Qui pensamo nei secoli"* ("Here, we think in centuries") is no longer acceptable as a non sequitur now that centuries of change are being telescoped into decades. Revolutions do not stop once they have gained momentum.

At a luncheon where I intended to draw some important French and Dutch bishops and experts, a kind of autopsy was being performed on this astonishing second session. How was it possible that, at the end of the session, the spirit that permeated the vast majority of bishops had not clearly prevailed? Exactly how had it been obstructed by the still entrenched minority of the rear guard? Why was it still entrenched? It had been repeatedly suggested that Pope Paul should have intervened to express the consensus of the majority. Paul had remained silent.

"He let us down," one *peritus* said bitterly. "Pope John would have intervened after the clear vote of October 30. He also would have made sure that the chapters on religious liberty and on the Jews would be voted on. Instead, Paul prevented it."

Another expert agreed, and quoted from Carlo Falconi's famous article in *Il Espresso,* written at the time of Paul VI's coronation. Had Pope John not referred to Cardinal Montini as "Your Cardinal Hamlet?" Falconi called him "a seesaw of pros and cons, of affirmations coolly denied, of denials as promptly changed into affirmations . . . of silence as the most valued defense and of indecision posing as prudence."

"He is certainly a dual character," the *peritus* continued. "He is probably sincere when he proclaims his commitment to Pope John's ultimate aims. On the other hand, unlike Pope John, he has been

*Pope Paul VI
remained silent ...*

part of the Curia for thirty years. Perhaps he was confident, so long as he was absent from Rome, that this qualified him to deal with it effectively. Had he not started out serving advance notice on the Curia that it was going to be put into its place? Couldn't it be that, once returned to the Vatican atmosphere, he could not detach himself after all, that old reflexes took over, and that he succumbed again to the old rules of the game?"

"Don't blame him for everything!" a third theologian exclaimed passionately. "It was not Paul but John who saddled us with an unworkable Theological Commission and an impossible chairman." "True," admitted the first. "But it is Paul who maintained him in power and disregarded requests for the formation of new commissions more in harmony with the spirit of the Council. He compromised: no new commissions! Just enlarge the old ones and keep the same chairmen who have the whip hand over a majority they don't even understand!"

"Give him time. You ask too much at once. Pope Paul has a long time before him," an old priest interjected mildly.

"Don't blame the Pope. Blame *us!*" cried a young Dutch bishop. "Blame us bishops! Did we make it clear that we were ripe for co-government with the Pope? Did we organize ourselves so that the voices of the majority could be heard as such? It is all well and good

[183]

to make fine progressive speeches, to make individual attacks on the Curia. We were given a charter at the start of the Council. We did not use it. We should have formed organs that clearly demonstrated our capacity to take over many of the responsibilities of the Curia. We did not organize. Why should Pope Paul take the initiative? He gave it to us. If we can't use it, we have only ourselves to blame for a regressive Church. We talked, but did not act. We swallowed every promise given by those who we knew never keep promises. It is we who ruined this session, the Council, and perhaps the Church."

French Episcopate at Conference

The solemn closing session was a repetition of the cesaro-papal pomp of the Coronation, as if to demonstrate that, after all those references to the "Church of the poor" and the emphatically expressed desire for reform, business would go on as usual, that triumphalism was not dead and that the forces of conservatism were for the moment in the ascendancy.

Yet it was as if the glitter had gone dull, the brilliance had dimmed, the lights in the Basilica had lost candlepower, the choirs were muffled, the helmets had tarnished, the uniforms had become threadbare.

The pope who at the opening of this second session had walked into St. Peter's as a bishop among bishops arrived on the *sedia gestatoria,* the *flabella* of ostrich feathers waving. He looked tired and drawn under the high white miter, as if he were undergoing an ordeal. Anxious to draw him from close by, I tried to sneak up to a grandstand reserved for Roman nobles. A tremulous chamberlain with a hearing aid stopped me, notwithstanding my official black and my monocle.

"Qu'est-ce que vous allez faire là-haut?" he asked menacingly.

"Pardon, mon cher monsieur," I said, *"je suis dessinateur."*

"Ah, vous êtes Sénateur," the old man said, switching on a most charming smile. He bowed from his Spanish waist and gestured me up on the tribune.

In the top row a simple priest was sitting. I sat down next to him. The old man in ruffles asked the priest for his ticket. "I am sorry," he said severely, waving the priest away arrogantly, "this is reserved for the Roman patriciate."

"Excusez-moi, cher monsieur," I interrupted him. "Are you aware that you are chasing *'un des esprits les plus nobles'* of the Catholic Church? *Permettez-moi de vous présenter le Père de Lubac."*

The little man vanished. Père de Lubac turned his kindly eyes toward me and studied my face.

"Have we met?" he asked.

"Never. But I drew you yesterday when you spoke at Domus Mariae. I have long admired your writings," I said, and showed him his portrait in my sketchbook.

When Pope Paul knelt during the Consecration I saw his head uncovered for the first time. It was imposing, square, and bald. A surprisingly large, pale, professorial skull dwarfed the small, compressed features beneath it: sensitive, enigmatic, disciplined. His thin mouth, half hidden by the curved nose, was drawn into a line that curved downward and inward as if it never intended to utter speech again.

The Master of Ceremonies, Archbishop Dante, looked very old and as if on the verge of unconsciousness; the second master of

R. Père Henri de Lubac

ceremonies, Capoferri, was swaying on his feet, his deeply walled eyes staring dead into space. The ceremony was endless and tiresome, but I had my sketchbook. More formal votes were taken on the liturgical and communications decrees. The Pope's closing address was proclaimed in a flat, precise voice to an audience that was fatigued, disenchanted, and apathetic.

In cautious Vaticanese, strikingly in contrast with his opening allocution, Paul VI gave a factual account of the achievements of the second session. He was pointedly mute about the issue of collegiality, nor did he refer to the bishops' rights, the ecumenical schema, the chapters on religious liberty and the Jews; yet he did not close any doors. He said that "questions would be subjected to deeper and thorough examination"; he hoped for "directives to guide biblical, patristic, and theological studies . . . by every good, modern scientific tool," and he called the Church "a religious society, a community of prayer . . . composed of people with a flourishing interior life."

If Pope Paul was not exactly indulging in revolutionary revelations, neither was he precisely speaking the language of the frozen orthodoxy. Was he really just waiting for an organized, authoritative, purposeful majority to rout the entrenched minority? He most definitely would not do it for them.

Neither could he be expected to dismantle impulsively the immense, interlocking organizational structure of the Church before replacements were ready.

Yet—in promulgating the decree *De Sacra Liturgia,* which had been approved by a vote of 2,147 to 4, he used a formula especially significant if one realizes that this was the first conciliar promulgation since that of 1870: "Paul, the Servant of the Servants of God *in union with the Fathers of the Council."* Did not this sound like a de facto confirmation of collegiality?

A wave of slowly increasing, incredulous excitement swept through St. Peter's when Paul VI announced to his carefully unprepared audience the sensational news of his forthcoming trip to the Holy Land, the first successor of Peter to return to Jerusalem since Peter left it.

Even before leaving St. Peter's I heard the plan skeptically questioned. Did it really mean that the outcome of the second session was felt to be so disastrous that a public relations move was necessary? Could this pilgrimage-by-jet be a device to take the spotlight off the Council and concentrate it once more on the papacy? Was it a sop to the Jews for having dropped the declaration which—none too soon after nearly two thousand years—was to lift the deicidal curse from them, that hunting license for Catholic anti-Semites, which the Council of Trent had unsuccessfully attempted to remove?

Other voices asserted that the Pope's journey represented a great new initiative to establish direct, personal contact with the Eastern Orthodox world, which had not been represented at the Council, a further step in the Joannine plan to throw open the doors of the Church to the world.

There was nothing to do now but go home and wait till the third session. Another critical nine months of gestation had come. The third session—it could hardly be the last—might yet bring a true updating, liberate the Church from its dilemma of choice between openness and closedness, between rigid authoritarianism and freedom. The new importance of the Orientals might help to break this vicious circle in which freedom leads to some sort of Protestantism, the authority principle to curial tyranny, for a third principle is the Orthodox concept of *Sobornost,* which transcends both: This expression indicates a community in the Holy Spirit without the abdication of differences. "The Holy Spirit does not act automatically when a Council is convened in accordance with arbitrary parliamentary regulations," says the great Russian theologian Khomiakov, "but a Council is where the Holy Spirit is working, where spiritual community exists as a supreme reality."

There was no doubt that, notwithstanding the power of the entrenched minority, this Spirit had been at work in the majority of bishops and that it would yet break through. That unique phenomenon John XXIII would not have lived in vain.

Before leaving Rome I still had a chance to visit Cardinal Bea in his simple study in the Via Aurelia.

I had heard the rumors that explained why he had not been heard from more in the last weeks of the session. The old cardinal, who stood for all the things John XXIII had stood for, had apparently been silenced at last by the conservative coalition. His ecumenical schema had been mutilated and he was forced to declare in the Council that "only time had prevented the declarations on religious liberty and on the Jews from coming to a vote." I asked one of his collaborators: "Will this kill the old man?"

The *peritus* laughed. "Oh, you don't know him. It will give him a new lease on life! He thrives on obstacles!"

The eighty-three-year-old sage was sitting in his room. He looked better than he had for months. His smile was radiant and serene.

"Sit down here with me." He pointed to a settee.

"Don't worry," he said, with that unforgettable smile, waving his large, yellowed hands in the air. "*Aufgeschoben ist nicht aufgehoben.* . . . There were controversial points. Now there will be time to study the entire matter in the light of these points of resistance. We now know about them. Don't worry!"

And then we talked about my home town of Maastricht. He had once lived there, behind the high brick walls of the Jesuit College. Before I was born he had already moved on to Valkenburg, in the hills a few miles to the east, where he had taught at the Jesuit Seminary. Yes, he too had loved those hills on the border.

"I left Valkenburg in 1921," the Cardinal reminisced.

In my imagination, all at once, I saw the narrow platform of the Valkenburg train-stop; a youngish Jesuit in long skirts was climbing into the dull-green little train. I saw myself in a blue-serge sailor suit already sitting in the train, watching him struggle up the high steps with his heavy basket-valise and his wet umbrella. I was twelve years old in 1921. Was it not in those days that I thought my love for the Church had died?

Toward an End

CAPPA MAGNAS, albs and copes, surplices, amices, tunicles, chasubles, maniples, cottas, rochets, dalmatics, cassocks and mantellettas, mozzettas, palliums and stoles, birettas and miters once more filled a shiny, golden-purple Basilica of St. Peter. The mortal bodies of these few thousand naked men were covered with all this holy and venerable haberdashery.

I sat opposite St. Peter's statue; the black, shiny foot, kissed and polished out of shape by the lips of a million faithful, emerged from beneath the stiff, golden cloak.

After distributing his photographers, Tenente Martelli had made a sweeping gesture: "Sit wherever you want!"

The chamberlain on the tribune behind the observers was horrified. *"Sono mortificato,"* he pleaded, "but it is quite impossible for you to sit here." With a sketchbook, too! He was fifty and needle-thin, a face full of wrinkles behind twinkling glasses, his lace collar freshly starched, his nervous hands fluttering between the jeweled grip of his sword that constantly poked between his spindly legs and my nose. For he had to make it absolutely clear, this impossibility of my presence, in compelling Italian gestures.

His plump Sancho Panza, second in command, repeated the treble words and gestures in slower, basso manner. I sat down quietly and repeated that I had the "official permission." It was no use; the pantomime continued. Then a gendarme in a busby looked in our direction as I gestured an SOS. He came running up the tribune stairs, three at a time, with tinkling spurs, and declared that the *professore* had the permission. My thin knight now made a sweeping, resigned bow, this time again *"mortificato"* because he had assumed my unlawful entry, while Sancho Panza stood smiling at me sweetly and apologetically.

Four or five very aged *principessas, duchessas* and/or *contessas* were heaving themselves up the tribune steps, panting and hissing under their mantillas. The incident being closed, the knights started to push and pull the noble pilgrims up, meanwhile chattering encouragingly, seductively, and even bowing during their efforts. They kept on bowing and chattering as they pushed the ladies gently into their rightful places. They bowed, straight like jackknives, and —bowing being their life's achievement—they also showed that you can bow sideways and according to degrees of intimacy or respect, with your eyes rolled up or cast down, and even with your head charmingly turned, like a parakeet soliciting a seed. The ladies smiled old-fashioned measured smiles—withered seeds.

The Altar of the Confession, between Bernini's gigantic pillars,

. . . bowing and chattering . . .

had been completely rebuilt for the concelebration of the Mass that was to follow. It looked like a large, nearly square box, or an improvised dining table, simply set—six short candles, a crucifix in the center—for the celebration of the Last Supper.

The twenty-five hundred bishops were already in their seats, not white-mitered but in their simple violet mozzettas, the working clothes of the Council sessions. And although the Pope entered on the *sedia gestatoria,* preceded by the twenty-four bishops who would celebrate the Mass with him, it was a smaller, simpler *sedia gestatoria* and the ostrich-feather *flabella* were missing. Thus the tone was set for what was to follow: a stirring religious ceremony instead of a pageant of *Romanità.* As the *"Tu es Petrus"* resounded through the huge church, everyone realized that liturgical reform had really taken effect, that something had already radically changed in the Roman Catholic Church. The solitude of the Pope had vanished as he stood at the altar, facing the congregation, surrounded by his bishops, six on each side of the huge square altar. "Peter and the other Apostles" were *bringing* the sacrifice of the Mass, one in voice and one in gesture. Three large hosts were broken by three cardinals and distributed to the other concelebrants; a smaller host was raised by the Pope. The Consecration sounded from twenty-five mouths as though it came from one.

The Credo and the Lord's Prayer were recited by an entire congregation, deeply moved.

Without one word to justify or explain it, it seemed that Paul VI had demonstrated to all but the most refractory that collegiality —in one form or another—had become a fact and that the vote of October 30, 1963, had not been disregarded after all. Had the Church from having been an absolute monarchy become something more like a commonwealth?

The Pope's Latin allocution that followed was long and tedious. In the heat of the early September day, made lethal by the batteries of klieg lights of the television companies, an observer and a cardinal were seen to collapse and were discreetly carried away. The Pope sat immobile on his throne, reading his speech in a flat lawyer's voice which now and then broke in fatigue, until at the very end it rose in emotion.

The two assistants to the throne, the Princes Colonna and Torlonia, were standing at attention in their finery, plumed hats under their arms, their faces stony in their desperate determination not to melt, faint, or sway; Colonna looked the traditional nobleman with well-cut face and arrogant grimace, Torlonia boyish, constructed more for scooter than charger.

The Masters of Ceremony, Monsignors Dante and Capoferri, were standing between the princes and the papal throne. Archbishop Dante looked even thinner and more worried than usual, the eyebrows raised on his emaciated, sad face. It must have been very worrisome to this old man of tradition, all this newfangled liturgy. Last year he had insisted on calling the Protestant observers to Communion instead of the Catholic auditors. "Pope's orders," he had replied to Monsignor Willebrands, who could not dissuade him until Felici (the photographer, not the Secretary General) stuck his Rolleiflex in the old archbishop's ribs and said: "Look, Excellency, if *they* would go to Communion, we'd be about ready to call it a day!"

Capoferri, fat and swarthy, always fascinated me. He looks as worldly as an old, melancholy headwaiter in a pizzeria. As I was drawing him again, I saw him sway. The deep, pigmented rings under his eyes became even darker, his hand suddenly moved to his heart, his head fell forward, then he jerked it back. It had been too much for him. He was half led, half carried, down the altar steps, past Prince Pacelli, who was still standing in his Noble Guard uniform but getting greener and greener under his golden, horse-tailed helmet until he too was replaced and could recover in the wings.

The congregation was fidgeting as the Pope read page after page of his address. He mentioned collegiality, but for every time he used the word he emphasized primacy a few times more, until the insistence on the intactness of the pronouncements of Vatican I became monotonous in its repetitiousness, grating on the nerves of Protestant observers and Catholic progressives alike. A Pacellian style of oratory had replaced the Roncallian style of communication, first in the Encyclical *Ecclesiam Suam,* now in the opening speech to the third session of Pope John's Council. In deploring modern atheism, Pope Paul could hardly fail to realize, as do huge numbers of people—both in and outside of the Church—the deeper causes that had contributed to the momentum of anticlericalism, secularism,

Pope Paul flanked by Msgrs. Dante & Capoferri

and communism in the traditionally Catholic countries, causes intimately connected with Church history, with the all too intimate ties between the Church and the ruling classes, its indifference to urgent problems of hunger, war, and birth control, ingrained habits of intimidation and tyranny only now very reluctantly abandoned by the Curia. Was the much decried triumphalism being replaced by a new style of self-satisfaction? Such myopia would be in contradiction to Pope Paul's earlier statements. Yet how to explain his renewed insistence on formulas of reunion that implied "return" to the Roman fold?

He could not possibly ignore the new reality: Rome was no longer a fixed point. It had become impossible to predict where a Rome-on-the-move would be found even a decade from now. Was he perhaps desperately trying to anchor as firmly as possible to his own authority this bark of St. Peter's, which after having been stranded on sandbanks for centuries, had now definitely chosen the dangerous open sea?

At last the long speech ended. The *Veni, Creator Spiritus,* imploring the help of the Holy Spirit, sounded through the Basilica. The Pope took his seat on the *sedia* and was lifted up to be carried back to his rooms. Immediately in front of me the *sedia* stopped for a long moment, waiting for the procession to form. The Pope was greeting the individual non-Catholic observers in the row in front of me. His face had changed, however. He looked relieved, as if a huge burden had been taken off his back. Sitting on the ludicrous, archaic apparatus, he looked happy and human. His smile was not sweet-and-sour now, but genuine and warm. Again, for a flash, a pope's eyes had met mine, and in that flash I "saw" Pope Paul.

I saw an utterly serious man, highly complex, tormented by an exceptional intelligence: contemplative and cautious, cerebral but sensitive and not heartless. A man hesitant and reluctant in reaching decisions, formulating them only when hard-pressed, formulating them, if at all possible, not in words but in symbolical acts like this concelebration, like his Palestine pilgrimage: symbolical acts allowing of interpretations with more latitude than words will permit.

Keenly aware of the moods of others, sensing the full danger of the ever-widening gulf between two factions that threaten to split his Church in two, he sees that his is the impossible task of reconciling what appears to be more and more irreconcilable.

The man on the *sedia gestatoria* has been part of the complex machinery of Vatican diplomacy on its highest level for three decades. He can underestimate neither its subtlety nor its ruthlessness. However much convinced of the ultimate soundness of Pope John's aims, he feels that he cannot afford in his position and character to use a single imprudent word that may frighten and further estrange the rear guard. As pope he feels bound to preserve to the utmost the organizational soundness and structure of the Church of which he is not only the spiritual head, but also the chief executive.

Painfully aware of the lack of communication between theological and ordinary twentieth-century language, he apparently feels, in contrast to Pope John, that he has no choice but to speak the theological language. Yet he has not hindered, but encouraged, others to continue their scientific research in matters of biblical exegesis, liturgical reform, comparative religious studies, and theological reformulations, work that must inevitably lead to the creation of a new language of understanding between Church and world.

A man sincerely Christocentric in his faith, split down the center by doubts and fears—his darting eyes betray him—wishing to place all emphasis on the central message of the Church as expressed by its Founder in both His life and His words, yet liable to make it more papocentric than ever in his compulsion to be all things to all men.

Utterly fearful of lowering the Church in the eyes of the faithful on all their levels of understanding and culture, Paul has nevertheless humbly admitted its sinfulness; he has left it to others to specify these sins, that bigotry, inquisition, forced conversion, and persecution, those ineffaceable blots for which penance is due and punishment is certainly received every day. He speaks in deeds as in the Concelebration, the rehabilitation of banished theologians, the downgrading of the Congregation of Rites in the execution of liturgical reform—and hence of the Curia—the addition of progressive cardinals to the Holy Office, the symbolical admission to the Council of a few laymen, and later even of women auditors. It is clear that this pope feels that, pressing as the reforms of the Church are, desperate as is the urgency to update the language of its central message, he must give his bishops, his priests, his laity, and even himself time to absorb and digest it all after four centuries of immobility and stagnation.

The man I saw then was very much Paul VI, not the mere successor of John XXIII. Not a Sign, not a Prophet, not a bodhisattva bestowing blessings, but a struggling, fearful man, an expert, a diplomat, obsessed—maybe against his very grain—with his duty to reconcile the old and the new, the familiar dead letter and the dangerous newborn spirit, the prophecy and the bureaucracy, the yogis and the commissars. Would Paul, not John, prove to be the transitional figure to an entirely new manifestation of the universality of his Church, or could he, in his ambiguity and fear, be the pope of the impressive, but too transparent, gestures, the pope of the missed opportunity?—the man who, overestimating the intellect —so much cheaper a commodity than the heart—trying to estrange no one, estranged them all?

The next day, the fifteenth of September, 1964, was the first working day of the third session, and it immediately set its mood—a mood totally different from that of the first session, and even more different from that of the second session, with its difficulties and filibusters. The power of the moderators, which during the second session had been disappointingly weak and in constant conflict with the other leading organisms, seemed immediately confirmed, without spectacular changes in either personnel or rules. No doubt, some pointed directives had been received from the papal desk. Even the bouncy Archbishop Felici now seemed to be the willing servant of the moderators; he tried only a few unsuccessful tricks. He was all spinechilling joviality.

The rear guard kept suspiciously quiet. Exhaustion or *drôle de guerre?* The future would show. The Council Fathers had again met as old acquaintances. The fundamental attitudes of all were known, so that without further exploration natural affinities could be reinforced and alignments reconstituted. They had digested two sessions, studied hard, and had become professionals instead of amateurs. It was as if twenty-five hundred country doctors, rigid in their routines, had been forced to take a rigorous postgraduate course taught by the greatest specialists in every discipline. The postgraduate course had done even more for them. Instead of brief periodical visits to Rome, where they were received—country cousins trembling in carefully polished shoes—by the Pope and his supercilious bureaucracy, they had now seen the Vatican machinery at work in close-up, had smelled the musty offices and seen the curial bureaucracy involved in its all too human activities, intrigues, and subterfuges. They would not soon forget it, and in the long run this might be the result of the Council most dangerous for the status quo.

All the sensations of novelty had gone, the jokes of the first session were pointedly absent; they had been replaced by a great sense of dedication and urgency. The de facto acceptance of the principle of collegiality in the opening ceremony had done more than any speech to encourage the bishops in becoming involved more consciously and intimately with every utterance of the Council.

It was not that the split between "progressives" and "conservatives" had been healed, but there was now a huge attractive majority, and a small, tactically powerful but obviously obsolete rear guard, more machine than faction. Even the Holy Office had prudently dele-gated or allowed one of its staunchest members—its second in com-mand, Archbishop Parente—the task of defending collegiality, al-though he emphasized that he spoke not for the Holy Office but for himself.

The attempts to go against Pope John's wish and to make this a doctrinal instead of a pastoral council by, for instance, petrifying dogmatic Mariological pronouncements, such as the term "Mediatrix of all Graces," was quickly defeated.

The Council seemed to be not merely in a pastoral but even in a prophetic mood; instead of laying down a few general principles as face-saving devices and spending their time at the coffee-bars, leav-ing the interpretation to postconciliar commissions, the bishops in their speeches, and especially the votes in their consistent near-unanimity, signified a determination to come to grips with all prob-lems presented. The conciliar commissions, apparently, were at last lubricated energetically and were turning at top speed to consider and process the verbal and written interventions made during the debates in order to facilitate early votes. Simultaneously, the debates were going on and votes *iuxta modum* (under reservation of pro-posed modification) made further adjustments to the wishes of mem-bers feasible, without holding up the voting on the principles themselves.

In this manner the discussions on the "Eschatological Character of the Church" and on the Virgin Mary were finished the first week, and at the same time chapters debated with great bitterness in the previous sessions were adopted with quasi-unanimity.

It began to appear possible that after the all-important declara-tions on religious liberty, on the Jews, and seven other short schemata had been discussed, the eagerly awaited Schema XIII, "The Church in the Modern World" would still be debated at this session. Here, after all, were the products of the Council that not only the Catholic world but even more so the non-Catholic world were truly interested in. They were to establish its *aggiornamento* and even more: its good faith.

It seemed obvious to all from whence the impetus was coming.

A press conference by the Pope's personal theologian, Bishop Carlo Colombo, had made it clear: "Under many aspects," the Bishop said, "the actual situation of the Church is absolutely new.

The Presidium and the Moderators

We only have to recall the population explosion and the consequent problem of providing Christian formation for immense masses. There is also the development of national consciousness and of cultural consciousness in the so-called mission countries. The Church believes in the presence within herself of a supernatural principle, the Holy Spirit, whose power is always capable of 'renewing the face of the earth' . . . providing the Church makes it possible for Him to exert all this renewing force."

It seemed, then, that all the schemata would be adopted, if only in weakened, compromise form, as, for example, in the vote on the reestablishment of the diaconate, where married men were acceptable as deacons, but marriage was forbidden to young men after ordination.

Monsignor Colombo again made himself heard during the debate on religious liberty. He called the declaration on religious liberty of "extreme importance . . . if it does not succeed, it will be the end of all dialogue. It is not enough that we give it a general character as if the Church seeks a compromise between its verities and pastoral necessity; it has to be rooted in doctrine." And he went on to argue for the "natural right to search for the truth," from which he concluded that not only freedom of research but freedom to communicate this research is a right, "not a necessary evil, but a good."

Was this not Pope Paul indirectly speaking to the Council? The

Msgr. Colombo in conversation with Msgr. Edelby

interventions of Cardinals Ritter and Meyer, Archbishop Hurley, Bishops Wright and Garonne were all unequivocal, prophetic, and courageous. It was a feast of pure reason and pure charity in a St. Peter's which had heard very different sermons. A few, old dissenting voices crackled an echo of old inquisitors, long stilled, who could be faintly heard turning in their graves after Cardinal Cushing thundered: "Throughout her history, the Catholic Church has ever insisted on her own freedom in civic society and before public powers. That same freedom in civic society the Church has ever insisted on for herself and her members she now also champions for other churches and their members, indeed for every human person." He was loudly applauded and the black African Bishop Zoa of Cameroun added: "It is absolutely necessary that religious liberty be doctrinally and not merely pragmatically justified . . . by the absolute dignity of the human person, created in God's image, and by solemnly rejecting the so-called right of using coercion on people . . . should a concrete possibility of practicing such coercion ever again present itself."

Pope John should have heard this! I could see him sitting in front of his closed-circuit TV set, looking at those twenty-five hundred bishops, some clever, some dense, some fast, some slow, some learned, some ignorant. He would have seen the white wings of the Dove hovering above the nave of St. Peter's and tears of joy would have been streaming from those eyes that had seen the great vision. . . .

During the ceremony in which the relic of the head of St. Andrew —it had been held in "safekeeping" in the Vatican for five hundred years—was to be returned to the Greek Orthodox Church in a gesture of brotherliness, I was sitting behind the cardinals and watched these poor seventy- and eighty-year-old men, wrapped in yards and yards of purple silk, struggle up the high steps to their seats as they had to do every morning at eight thirty. The bent, eighty-three-year-old Cardinal Bea was amongst the most agile. Ottaviani was sitting a little in front to the right, Roberti to my left, while younger men, like Léger, Rugambwa, Koenig, and Confalonieri, sat on the much more accessible lower tiers. A terribly decrepit cardinal of ninety had his seat immediately in front of me. He was supported up the steps by two other ancients, and as he clambered, trembling, to his seat, his dark eyes glazed with age stared helplessly into space, unfocused, like a baby's. The redoubtable Dominican Cardinal Browne sat a few seats away, his great, totally institutionalized, near-inhuman head consisting of trillions of tiny wrinkles, the eyes hidden beneath drooping, parchment eyelids.

How could these very old men be expected to take part in the tremendous mutation the world and the Church within it were going through? Was not one of the problems the Council struggled with a geriatric one? The poor little cardinal in front of me continued to pant and tremble. Through his purple he smelled like a very old, sick animal. Cardinal Marella started the Mass, but I could not follow it. I was watching in astonishment these old cardinals surrounding me. After all these decades, there was nothing of routine in their participation in the Mass. Ottaviani, his eyes closed in recollection, had become majestic and nobly beautiful. Koenig radiated a deep quiet, Léger intense fervor. All these faces were absorbed in a great Presence.

Deep below me, a little to the right, on a simple throne, the Pope was sitting immobile, as if dead. His face was expressionless as he sat facing the severe, antique reliquary, containing the Apostle's head, but I saw his eyes again restlessly sweeping over the Basilica, like those of a nervous hostess continually making sure all was going according to plan. He looked frail and small, as if crushed under the weight of the cardinals towering above him. Tomorrow the relic would be taken to Greece by the venerable old Augustin Bea. After the kiss of peace with Patriarch Athenagoras in Jerusalem, the Pope had made a second great gesture to the Orthodox Church.

The declaration on the Jews had been watered down in the intersession, as had been rumored all along. Cardinal Bea read the *relatio*. He must have been highly pleased with what followed. Achille Cardinal Liénart, who reserves his interventions for great occasions, was moved to make his first intervention of this session. He demanded that the declaration should specifically clear the Jewish people of the collective guilt of deicide, so often through the centuries made a pretext for persecution and pogrom: "All Christianity," he said, "is grafted on the olive tree of the Jewish people." "The Son of God chose to be born Jewish; Mary and the Apostles were Jewish. I demand that the original declaration be restored. That is a minimum. It is a demand of justice, not just of charity. . . .

Cardinal Koenig of Vienna

The Council of Trent moreover says explicitly that all men are in some way deicides."

Cardinal Lercaro stressed the essential tie between Catholics and Jews: "I think there should be dialogue with the Jews in order to help us to understand the Bible better." Cardinal Léger: "Our origins are Jewish. The Jewish people must enjoy a special dignity in Christian thought."

Cardinal Cushing bellowed: "Catholics have not behaved toward Jews as they should have. They are often guilty of indifference, sometimes of crimes. We have to ask forgiveness for our faults." Also Cardinal Koenig called for the first version to be reinstated: "If amongst the faithful there is anti-Semitism, it is because of misinterpretation of Scripture."

They were followed by the late Cardinal Meyer, by the Americans O'Boyle and Leven, by the saintly Descuffi of Smyrna, by Mendes Arcéo of Cuernavaca, by Seper of Yugoslavia, by that young mountaineering bishop of the Alps and of the spirit, Elchinger of Strasbourg, and by Bishop Daem of Antwerp, a man so like John XXIII in appearance, mildnes, and good humor that I saw John interposed all the time I was drawing his portrait. They all openly deplored past misinterpretation of the Gospels, which had served to rationalize anti-Semitism and wished to ask forgiveness for all the sufferings caused the Jewish people throughout the centuries. Only Cardinal Tappouni in the name of six Eastern patriarchs, themselves members of minorities in Moslem countries, demanded suppression of the document on grounds of inopportunity, while disclaiming all anti-Semitism.

But behind the scenes, the phony war had now ended and the diehards were fighting in earnest. A violently anti-Semitic brochure had been mailed to the bishops, accusing a "conspiracy of international Jewry and Free-Masons" of perverting the doctrine, using "converted Jews like Cardinal Bea, Bishop Mendes Arcéo and Monsignor Oesterreicher" to accomplish this. Cardinal Ruffini complemented it with a speech, repeating anti-Semitic canards, predating Hitler by a generation. It was known that at the same time reactionary prelates were working on Paul VI, trying to frighten him into believing that adoption of the declarations would ruin the Church and might even unchain a third world war. The intrigues went so far that Secretary Felici announced on October 13, under so-called orders of the Pope, that the declaration on religious liberty would be restudied by a special commission, of which the majority consisted of known foes of the declaration, and taken away from the Secretariat for the Promotion of Christian Unity. The trick did not succeed. Seventeen cardinals wrote to the Pope to acquaint him with the unprincipled use of his name to cover up maneuvers that could nullify the spirit and the rules of the Council. It was even rumored that Archbishop Felici was forced to apologize to Cardinal Bea for what, with Roman euphemism, was called an "erroneous statement." The cardinals also charged that there was a move afoot to cut to one insignificant paragraph the eight-hundred-word Declaration on the Jews and non-Christians and to rewrite the Declaration on Religious Liberty, both overwhelmingly supported on the Council floor. They also revealed that the rear guard was threatening to curtail the share of the bishops in the "full authority" of the Church by dropping the word "full" and was trying to force an end to the Council in order to avoid discussion of Schema XIII, "The Church in the Modern World," which would have to touch on "dangerous" subjects like birth control, mixed marriages, nuclear weapons, and conscientious objection. It was now being quipped that the difference between a progressive and a conservative was that the progressives found "the pill" less dangerous than the hydrogen bomb and so differed from the conservatives, who could manage to live with the hydrogen bomb but found "the pill" immensely dangerous.

It was clear by now that the Council as such had opted for openness and for a Joannine Church, relevant to the real world, open to all, plausible to all. A real breakthrough of this new spirit in official decisions could only be blocked by tactics smelling more of the witches' cauldron than of conciliar sanctity. This clever obstruction did not come from a sanely conservative minority, not from what was vaguely called the Curia, but from a well-oiled machine consisting of diehard cardinals—the names Cicognani, Antoniutti, Siri, and Browne were constantly whispered as forming the brain trust—it was assisted by a small group of Italian and Spanish reactionary bishops like Bishop Carli of Segni as the tools, and Archbishop Felici as the visible and audible representative. They were well placed around the Pope to exert constant pressure on him by persuasion, threat, and intimidation. Even a pope cannot afford a strike of his departmental chiefs. Their cause had lost even a ghost of a chance on the floor of the Council, where the diffidence of the bishops born and raised in awe of the central power, trained in an unquestioning obedience that had slowed their defensive reflexes, had been their only ally.

Archbishops Pericle Felici and Enrico Dante

In the discussion on Mary, on the nature of the Church, on religious liberty, and on the Jews, it had become clear for all to see how deep the soul-searching of this Council-in-mutation had gone, how close it had drawn to the suffering world and to the message of its Founder's life, how it had been led to that openness, fairness, and charity that had moved the prophet who had called it.

The Council had taken up a subject that had caused the most dramatic conflict of the first session, when after the debate on the liturgy it began discussing a schema called "The Sources of Revelation," which attempted to assess the roles of scripture and tradition in the transmission of the essentials of Christian faith. After days of bitter debate, a vote was taken that showed that the majority—though not the required two-thirds majority—rejected the schema as a basis for drawing up a constitution. Pope John had intervened and, in the spirit of the Council, withdrawn the schema, ordering a mixed commission, to which Cardinal Bea was added, to prepare a new draft. This, in its turn, was amended by many written objections in the intersession. It even received a new title. During the second session, the schema had been presumed dead, when Pope Paul revealed in December, 1963, that it would be discussed in the third session.

During the Reformation it was the Protestants who held that Scripture was the key to the nature of Christianity. The Council of Trent returned this uncompromising attitude by asserting that the "deposit of Faith" was preserved by *Scripture AND Tradition*. Conservatives on both sides of the doctrinal gulf hardened their attitudes, until in the nineteenth century Catholics began to see tradition as a means to better understanding of Scripture and Protestants began to rehabilitate tradition. In the new schema, a new, "mystical" element is admitted, which breaks with the habit of flawless logical deduction from propositions held to be true. It sees the message of the Gospel as what Abbot Butler called a "perpetual reannouncement of the Word, lived and spoken by Christ, one in nature with God, as a matter not simply for theological deductions but for loving and unceasing meditation." Or, to quote the Dutch theologian Schillebeeckx: "A living reality, not a mere transmission of intellectual knowledge." In the new schema, the Church admits for the first time that dogmas can evolve and that in the course of history "our knowledge of revelation can increase."

Cardinal Rugambwa

Suddenly I was jerked out of my concentration on the happenings in the Council. My exhibition of "Council Drawings" had arrived from the museum in Holland where it had last been shown. It was to open in Rome under the auspices of the Dutch Documentation Center for the Council in the same Palazzo Doria Pamphilj where I had now found hospitality for a fourth time.

When the eighty drawings were on the walls, the show was opened by the shy African Cardinal Rugambwa, after Bishop Wright of Pittsburgh had introduced it to the press. The great French Dominican, Père Chenu, gave the opening talk. He was one of that foursome of forerunners of the Council who had suffered persecution by Rome for decades, and who had at last been rehabilitated. It seemed incredible to me, and I was deeply moved to see Père de Lubac, against whose school of thought Pius XII had thundered a special encyclical, Père Yves Congar, Hans Küng, the humane Yugoslav Bishop Seper, the rebellious English Archbishop Roberts, Cardinal Alfrink, the Soviet observer Vitali Borovoj, as well as Professor Oscar Cullmann—the great peacemaker between the churches—standing there, looking at my drawings, involved, a little puzzled, and amused. Even Father Eugene was present and the man who had helped me so much, the shy Bishop Klooster of Surabaja. The Prince and Princess Doria had also come, as visitors in their own house.

Vitali Borovoj, in his tall purple headgear, icons and crosses decorating his broad chest, was looking at a drawing of an ancient cardinal:

"No goott," he said to me. "It is a lie. You coult not have caught him awake!" The Pope's personal chamberlain, Monsignor Del Gallo, with his keen, aristocratic head, looked with amusement at the "Pilgrims" and said with a twinkle: *"De temps en temps vous êtes méchant!"* "That, Monseigneur," I said, "is what I call dialogue."

After the opening, I drove a few bishops to their hotels. As we passed the Holy Office, one of them whispered in my ear, "Look out, boy, step on it. They might be gunning for me and hit you!"

In the Council sessions, where I was allowed to draw in those days, the atmosphere was relaxed and joyous, fraternal and optimistic. In the coffee-bars I heard high-spirited discussion. There was general gaiety after Bishop Carter of Sault Sainte Marie, Canada, said that the "document on the laity" had been "conceived in sin, the sin of clericalism," and demanded the participation of laymen in the construction of a new schema. The same day another Council Father, Archbishop Kozlowiecki (Rhodesia) dared to call clericalism "the number one enemy of the Church," and Archbishop D'Souza said: "The people of God is not totalitarian. Let us treat the laymen as

R. Père N. Chenu

our brothers, for in the eyes of God they are the equals of the bishops."

It was not a spirit of rebellion, but one of joy and liberation that blew through St. Peter's during the third session. All problems were discussed spiritedly and freely. It was a very special sensation to walk with Cardinal Alfrink or Professor Cullmann into Bar Jonah or Bar Abbas, the overcrowded, narrow corridors that had been transformed into coffee-bars, into which the bishops streamed and jostled each other every morning while less important statements were droned out in the *aula*. No photographer had ever penetrated into these holiest of holies and I wondered very much if any layman ever had. As a black-coated sardine among purple-and-mauve ones, I even drew there and was looked at with some bafflement, but without interference.

In these days Cardinal Alfrink obtained permission for me to attend sessions provided I did not put up my easel right in front of the president's table and I could hear Patriarch Maximos IV Savegh, the hieratic ancient, speak bluntly in his beautiful French about the Oriental schema. In his eighty-seventh year, Maximos had left behind him all need to use guarded language. He sounded younger than any other man in the Council. "The Patriarchate," he said, "is not simply an honorific title. One should not cover us Oriental patriarchs with honor, and treat us afterwards as subalterns whose authority depends in every detail on the Congregations of the Roman Curia." After the forced latinization of the Uniat churches he called "the respect" of which the schema speaks "pure irony."

Archbishop Heenan of Westminster, the great adversary of "the pill," the man who had been taken to task by the press for calling Pope John "no genius," and who, wishing to deflate this "myth," made an intemperate attack on the *periti* in general and on the highly respected moral theologian Father Häring in particular, and was tongue-lashed on the Council floor by the Benedictine Abbot Reetz of Beuron. The next day the joke was all over Rome: Monseigneur Heenan was seriously ill. He was suffering from "acute peritonitis" after swallowing a "häring" and the prognosis was bad; he had refused all "pills" and had even taken a too-large dose of "Benedictine."

By now I felt completely part of it all: I had drawn innumerable

Council Fathers; I had drawn the Council in action and had become identified with it. When I had first come to Rome, moved by the spirit of John XXIII, I was an outsider looking in. Now I felt at least as much a part of it as the observers on their tribune. As I stood drawing in a corner, bishops came by—the faces I remembered but the names had escaped—and asked me how I was doing or drew my attention to "something I must not forget to draw." One of these dragged me to the confessional of the Council, where a monk was hearing the Council Fathers' confessions. Cardinal Agagianian, walking in, saw me drawing the scene and, raising his heavy eyebrows, gave me a strange, bewildered look.

A spiritual revolution had taken place within the ancient Church, a revolution that is essentially anti-institutional. Dozens of bishops sounded more anticlerical than a nineteenth-century liberal diehard. The Church had entered upon an unprecedented adventure of the spirit, a new attitude toward man's condition and his place on earth and in the cosmos, a true religious explosion of a strength and gentleness that might undermine modern man's materialistic and mechanistic habits of thought. It was as if a mystical revelation of oneness was going to replace all juridical obsession. A new, joyous affirmation of life and openness to life had emerged, in complete contrast with the traditional Christian preoccupation with suffering, death, and the hereafter, bringing with it a new sense of solidarity with all beings on an earth in constantly creative evolution.

In just two years, notwithstanding all quarrels and intrigues at the organizational level, the great majority of what had arrived in Rome as a heterogeneous mass of bishops had become infused with a vision of the human condition and of human unity that once more made the Church universal and catholic instead of Roman and exclusive. It was now only struggling to transmit this vision in new words. The speeches on the Council floor had become ever more bold, profound, tolerant, and free. Who could have expected the great approval that swept St. Peter's when words like these were spoken:

CARDINAL RICKETTS: In the old days the word "spiritual" was synonymous with the flight from the temporal. Now we seek to place the spiritual within the temporal.

Bar Abbas at 11 a.m.

CARDINAL MEYER: The world is not only the means but the object of redemption. Not only man but the cosmos must be glorified. Let us think of the human order in function of the transfiguration that awaits it. In this light we should see all our present efforts, whether economical, social, or political.

BISHOP ELCHINGER: The Church does not seem to have the habit of thinking of its primordial concern: that man should be truly alive, for someone could say that sadness is seen as a Christian virtue . . . life is man's first duty, also that of the Christian . . . many Christians are contaminated with economic and biological idolatry. *The Church must save the transcendent quality of life,* the pastor must be a servant and defender of life. These problems must be treated not with professorial reasoning but with prophetic inspiration.

CARDINAL SILVA HENRIQUEZ: Let us start a dialogue with modern humanism. Contemporary atheism gets its force from its affirmation of temporal values. The Church should do the same. Only in this way can we come to an efficient collaboration with all men of goodwill. . . . We need a cosmic liturgy to really sing the glories of God.

This was the voice of the Council in the third session, which all the intrigues of a desperately rigid and deadly afraid, but politically powerful, remnant could never silence again. Where the rear guard had succeeded in blocking the main avenues, the Holy Spirit had humbly and joyously taken the back streets.

During the discussion of Schema XIII the world was listening to the Council. Subjects like the reform of the liturgy, collegiality, the education of priests did not excite it at all. Even religious liberty as a subject of discussion was interesting only because the Church had lagged one hundred and fifty years behind in what was no longer a problem in most of the world, ever since the French Revolution. In Schema XIII, "The Church in the Modern World," however, the Church was openly discussing matters of common concern. All scheming had failed to ban the discussion of the five "annexes" from the Council floor. Archbishop Felici had announced blandly that these "annexes" had a "purely private character and no conciliar value," until he was chastised by Cardinal Suenens, who made it clear that they were the work of an official commission of the Council, working on orders of the Coordination Commission, and that they would definitely be discussed. These "annexes" came to grips concretely with such subjects as marriage and family, economic and social life, the international community and peace. They were concerned with such subjects as the justification of war in our time, of ABC weapons, and of birth control. These were the very topics the men of the rear guard wanted to bury most thoroughly, and which they feared so much that they had tried to abrogate the Council in order to make their discussion impossible. But now Cardinal Alfrink could ask the question: "Can an atomic war be 'just' in any circumstances?" and Bishop Guilhem of Laval could state: "The ABC weapons have thrown the world into anxiety. They must be condemned as the supreme injustice to God and man."

During the discussion of marriage and the regulation of births, Cardinal Suenens could say: "There is another aim to marriage than mere procreation, and that is the intercommunion of persons. I beseech you, Fathers, let us not have another Galileo trial. One is enough."

Maximos IV warned the Council not to fall victim to a "psychosis

. . . a confessional in the Aula, with Cardinal Agagianian

Cardinal Suenens of Belgium

of celibates," and humorously implied that bishops were not the most competent experts on sex. On the Bomb he said: "How can we still speak of a 'just' war? What use are our pastoral efforts, if man must disappear? Let us reject the arguments of those who would decimate mankind under pretext of defending it." Another of Maximos IV's utterances was: "Let us change radically our way of teaching ethics. We are too legalistic. We are no longer dealing with a closed, absolutist society. We make the Friday fast an obligation for our faithful and say that absence from Sunday Mass is a mortal sin. This is not reasonable. Nobody believes us, even Unbelievers have pity on us. Modern man resents all coercion. John XXIII has said with much reason: 'We have not yet discovered the veritable demands of charity.'"

There was, of course, strong resistance from the conservative minority against all changes in the Church's attitude to birth control. The doctrinal side was defended by Cardinal Browne. Cardinal Ottaviani limited himself to a personal witness. The old man stood up with sad, half-blind eyes and said: "I am the eleventh child of a family of twelve children. We were poor. My father was a working-man. My parents never doubted Providence and notwithstanding our poverty it always came to our help."

He was very moving, that old man standing there, unable to understand the changed mentality of his Church and of the world around him, reminiscing about his childhood and recalling his parents.

Yet while voices of reason were sounding in the *aula,* the rumors of maneuvers behind the scenes were increasing. There were top-secret meetings of commissions, from which *periti* were barred. In the middle of bishops' conferences and observers' meetings, key figures were suddenly called to the phone and disappeared with worried faces. An atmosphere of suspicion developed. During a single week, as I was drawing three bishops I heard them speak enthusiastically about the progress and energy of the Council, but at the same time all three expressed their apprehensions of dark intrigues going on behind their backs—intrigues, as one of them put it, that "dishonor the Council and insult us." No one seemed to know where precisely to place the blame. There was a tendency to excuse the Pope, either as a prisoner or as a man too scrupulous to hurt anyone's feelings. But "they" were in bad faith; no one doubted it.

An article appeared in the diocesan newspaper of Lille. In it the Auxiliary Bishop of Lille, Monseigneur Dupont—a heavyset, kindly, peasantlike man in his sixties whom I had met one day at my exhibition with his two middle-aged sisters—wrote about the maneuvers of Monsignor Felici in trying to torpedo the Declarations on the Jews and on Religious Liberty: "The press, notwithstanding its usual discretion, has allowed us to guess something of that adventure. Some who pose as men of the Council are in reality but too inclined to do without it, to orchestrate everything without it and outside of it. Fortunately (in Latin, *feliciter*) they are dealing with a strong adversary. But when their batteries are unmasked these clever schemers quietly withdraw without fife and drum. Here the game is never definitely won. The watchword is to be awake, to be suspicious, ready for the counterattack. The climate is favorable to the *combinazione.* It is not for nothing that Machiavelli was born on this peninsula."

At a press conference Monsignor Helder Camara, Archbishop of Recife, Brazil, also praised the press just after it had been berated by the Press Committee of the Council: "The Church has no need of our pious lies!"

*Archbishop Helder Camara
of Recife, Brazil*

Helder Camara is a tiny man, all alive and all wrinkled. He is the apostle of the poor in poverty-stricken northern Brazil, and he had shocked the Council in its first session by suggesting the abolishment of all pomp, all purple, all golden crosses, and honorific titles. He is an actor, a mime, and a saint, who has to be experienced. He says: "We have to earn the right to speak the truth by our love. We in Latin America know that there are other causes for the obliteration of the human person than those that happen behind the Iron Curtain." And: "Since my childhood I have waited for this Declaration on the Jews. There is a man called Bea. He is a prophet and he makes us think of John XXIII." Helder Camara also said: "Science requires loyalty, humility, and patience. We, however, like to be pompous, behave as if we have the monopoly on truth and are judges and censors."

No wonder that the old monsignors of the Curia were enraged. The Holy Spirit was blowing where it listeth through the *aula*, through the press, too. But it was blowing uncomfortably hard!

The notorious Monsignor Romeo of the Congregation of Seminaries was quoted in the press as having called the Council "a sinister comedy by three thousand good-for-nothings with gold crosses on their chests, who, some of them, do not even believe in the Trinity or the Holy Virgin."

More ominous rumblings continued in the air. On October 29 it was learned that the text of the Declaration on Religious Liberty would remain with the Secretariat for Unity, but that "other bishops of the opposition had been invited to discuss it further." They were partly the same names as the ones mentioned in the Felici ultimatum to Cardinal Bea and protested by the seventeen cardinals in their famous letter. But now the move was in accord with the rules of the Council. Presumably differences would now be ironed out, and around the eleventh of November it was said that the Declaration had gone to press. It was not heard of again until too late. . . .

Notwithstanding all fears, the Council continued in high spirits. Pope John's three objectives were being brilliantly fulfilled: The Church was reforming itself (was there not an enormous majority in favor of collegiality?). The dialogue with the separated Christians was developing (was there not a crushing majority in favor of the Ecumenical schema?). The dialogue with the world was proceeding as well as could be expected (was not Schema XIII being discussed passionately, openly, and constructively?).

I lunched with Professor Cullmann at his favorite restaurant, Federico, just off the Via della Conciliazione. In a corner three German bishops were eating and enjoying their *vino bianco*. Federico, proud of his elegant clientele, was hopping around, making sure the *canneloni* were hot and the salad well mixed.

"It is going too well. I am scared," I said.

"You are a pessimist," Cullmann smiled, his eyes peering at me through his thick glasses.

"What do *you* think, Professor?"

"I saw the Pope last week for a full hour. He seemed relaxed and very pleased with everything. He asked me to write a report on a plan for an ecumenical institute he intends to found, and he gave me a marvelous present: the first Bible ever printed in Italian."

"Are you optimistic, then, about this session?"

Professor Cullmann was certain that the Declaration on Religious Liberty would be accepted. Of the Declaration on the Jews he was not so sure. Apart from that he said he was grateful that none of the decisions of the Council had closed any doors. "I agree, this is a negative gain," he smiled, "but don't forget that previous popes and previous councils closed many doors, and closed them forever, for their decrees cannot be repealed. In the wish not to close any doors this time any further there is an implied admission that this closing of discussion hinders further understanding of revealed truth. On the other hand, quite new doors have really been opened: in ecumenical thought, in the Declaration on Religious Liberty and on the non-Christian religions. Also, in the schema on the Church the formulation that the Church is "the people of God on its way" is new, and a point of view which opens the way to a dynamic theology. The text on collegiality is also a door which was opened, although I cannot share the assumption that the relationship of Peter to the other Apostles can be directly applied to that of the pope and the bishops. Don't take me wrong: I am not so satisfied with the texts themselves, they are typical compromise texts; the Holy Spirit is more visible in the general will to renewal than in the texts themselves. Without this will to reform, the texts can even be used to take steps backward, and often the biblical references are not the basis of the statements, but justifications added after the text has been decided upon. But the Council certainly has seriously and profoundly searched its soul. The changed mentality, the changed attitudes toward non-Catholics, toward laymen, no longer considered as "fuel for the ecclesiastical locomotive," toward women, toward priests, all these things are all great steps. For us Protestants most of this became self-evident long ago. But what it means to Catholicism we cannot even fathom."

Federico was clearing the table, solicitous and servile. The German bishops had left after bows and handshakes. It was late and I wanted to hear Hans Küng speak about "Veracity in the Church."

The library of the Palazzo Doria was so crowded half an hour before the beginning of Professor Küng's lecture that I went upstairs and listened to it in the recording room of the Dutch Broadcasting Company. There, an overflow audience of young priests and laymen followed every word passionately. Küng attacked all sins against veracity in the Church of today, the bad habit of never admitting past error, as in never having repealed Galileo's condemnation after hundreds of years. It did not admit error when at last it permitted the taking of interest, when the interpretation of the biblical story of creation and of original sin was changing, when the necessity of a papal state was abandoned. This, said Küng, is a habit resulting from an attitude of mind formed by a triumphalist doctrine of the Church on the one hand and the mentality of siege on the other. "Nothing is so damaging to the credibility of the Church in the modern world," he said, "as this compulsion to be silent, to circumvent or to confuse instead of honestly admitting the errors of the past. To err is human, to admit error is liberating, as truth is always liberating. By its sincerity the Council could regain some of the trust the Church has lost in the course of the centuries through its lack of veracity."

The young priests in the recording room went wild with enthusiasm. At every new point Küng made they acted as if they were watching a soccer match in which the home team made all the goals.

"The message of Jesus," Küng continued, "is a sharp protest against all kinds of unveracity, hypocrisy, and insincerity: the truth of the Gospels demands the veracity of the Church. The world does not ask the Church for theological theories about its state, its culture, its progress, achieved with, without, or against the Church. It does not expect from the Church that it propound the truth, but that it be the truth, exist as truth, be engaged in truth without compromise, not by offering abstract, theoretical affirmations, but by living the truth in its concrete and practical acts and decisions."

He indicated practical applications: "Let us give no more triumphalist directives to the press: our failings as well as our successes have to be public. Also, there should be more freedom in the Church. Let us abolish the Index, censorship, and other inquisitorial measures. Let us not just issue beautiful statements about love and marriage, but give a clear, honest, reasonable response to the question of birth control that does not put burdens on human shoulders of which we are not quite sure whether they are justified by God or just have to fit into our moral system; let there be a just representation of all the Churches in the Roman central authority."

The next morning, Küng's speech still ringing in my ears, I stood in the Vatican on the Cortile San Damaso. The Pope would receive the President of the new African state of Zambia. The *gendarmeria* was standing at attention in its Napoleonic gala uniforms: some forty men in busbies, white breeches, and patent-leather thigh-boots. A uniformed band was playing in the courtyard. Six Cadillacs and Buicks born in the middle thirties, the papal flag on their fenders, slowly left the small piazza to pick up the head of state and his retinue. When they returned, the door to the papal apartments was flanked by medieval knights, ruffled Spanish grandees, and Swiss guards. Nervous prelates in purple were gesturing at bellied gentlemen, covered with medals and adjusting their plumed bicorned hats.

Tenente Martelli shouted martial commands, trumpets blared, sabers were presented. The President of Zambia alighted from the ancient Cadillac in his African nightshirt. The Swiss, the grandees, the bicorned gentlemen stuck out their chests to capacity and stood at attention. The band started the papal hymn; it blew a few measures, stopped short grotesquely, and started all over again each time a Cadillac stopped to unload another dignitary. The monsignors put on fresh bows and new smiles in the same rhythm. It was fantastic to stand there in 1964 drawing the early nineteenth century in action. Then we suddenly relaxed for half an hour while the operetta continued inside. The Noble Guards had followed the President. Only two Swiss guards remained. The bicorned gentlemen were talking in one corner, the chauffeurs in another. The *gendarmeria* stood at ease. Martelli was talking to a grandee. A martial figure still at at-

The Gendarmeria Pontifica in full force

tention near the door said to me from the corner of his mouth, just under his immense busby, "Saw your show. Terrific! Draw me!"

Suddenly there was a shouted command. The drivers stopped their meeting under the arcade and ran to their antiques. The band started the papal hymn again, the guards drew their swords, the old gentlemen adjusted their plumed hats and pulled in their bellies in unison. The tall thin man in the African shirt climbed smiling into the Cadillac. It was all over in five minutes. Tiny Fiats drove up and the grandees folded themselves into them, cigarettes dangling, pulling their swords in last. I followed Martelli into his office.

"I'd like to draw you once more in that high thing," I said.

"Oh, please," he pleaded, "not now. It gives me a terrible headache. It seems they make a lighter, plastic model now. We have ordered a sample already."

As I walked down the *Scala Regia* a horde of three or four hundred people were climbing up the stairs, men in dark suits, women in mantillas, for the next audience. They looked like a convention of burgomasters or maybe wholesale meat packers. I knew they would have to wait long, for I had met the three directors of a record company, who would precede them to present the Holy Father with an album of their latest twenty-five records of sacred music in a white leather box, embossed with the papal arms. It would take at least twenty minutes.

I am not sure it was the same afternoon or that of the next day when Paul VI told his general audience: "The presence of the Pope, visible head of the Church, reminds all that in the Council there exists a sovereign, personal power with authority over the whole community gathered in the name of Christ." He went on to regret that "everywhere has spread a mentality of Protestantism and modernism which denies the need of an intermediate authority between the soul and God. 'How many men between God and me?' " he quoted Rousseau, whom he called "a famous epigone of that mentality."

Cold shivers ran over many Protestant and Catholic spines that night. "Someone put that speech under his nose," the optimists said. "Rousseau was not one of our Church fathers," scoffed a Protestant observer. . . . "He is overburdened, poor Pope Paul; he should have cancelled all audiences during the Council session," said one of our nuns charitably. "Yes, but he needs the contact with the people so much," said the sentimental one. "He cannot do without them, especially the little children." "He is in plain regression," muttered a learned Franciscan.

On Friday, November 6, 1964, Pope Paul would, for the first time, attend a routine Council meeting. The discussion of Schema XIII was interrupted. The draft of the Mission Schema would be read in the Council. It had been rumored for days that this draft was completely obsolete and would certainly be rejected.

During the endless Mass according to the Ethiopian rite, the Pope again sat on the small throne in the nave of St. Peter's facing the altar. A choir of Ethiopian priests sang the mysterious music, accompanied by drums and other percussion instruments. The rite, in Gheez, the Ethiopic equivalent of Church Latin, was obscure to the bishops, and it continued for more than an hour. The cardinals fidgeted, watching one another for cues when to kneel, rise, or sit down. Archbishop Dante nervously tugged at the Pope's sleeve to

Concelebration during a morning session

Cardinal Bea corrects his speech

prompt him, not quite sure himself. I was sitting behind Cardinal Bea, who was going to speak later in the name of the African and Asian bishops. He looked frighteningly frail and spent. As the other cardinals hesitatingly went through the required motions, discreetly yawning now and then or looking at each other quizzically, Cardinal Bea pulled out his handwritten speech at last and tremulously changed a word here and there, bent double over his paper.

At last the Mass ended. The Ethiopian bishops had made their last deep bows to the Pope, to the Patriarchs, to the Cardinals. The Pope was conducted to the table of the Presidium and took his place in the middle, where Cardinal Tisserant had made room for him. The President's chair had been raised a few inches above its usual level.

Pope Paul read a speech in which he congratulated Cardinal Agagianian on his draft for the schema on the Missions and said to the Council: "We think that you can easily approve this schema after the necessary perfections." Then he left the Basilica and Cardinal Agagianian related the schema. The first speaker to follow was Cardinal Léger. He severely criticized, if not disposed of, the draft. "What does this schema mean by a Central Commission of Evangelization which would work "with" the Propaganda Fide? Not 'with' but 'within,' becoming its supreme authority!"

Instead of talking collegiality, the bishops were putting it into action. Even against the Pope. The bishops and cardinals who followed Léger that day and the next condemned the schema as obsolete and inadequate. The missionaries were no longer to be the emissaries of the West; ecclesiastical colonialism had ended. *Basta!*

Who had misinformed Pope Paul and made him look foolish? The distance between Pope Paul and the Council had been increased again. The balance between the structure of which he is the guardian and the reality of the Spirit, which the bishops had been discovering in themselves and confirming in one another, was getting more precarious. Could this gap be closed? Was there not at the base of it a crisis in human consciousness, in which a "democratic" view of life and liberty was attempting to adapt itself to a centralized monarchism with all its secret machinations, unable to come to terms with it?

In St. Peter's I sat a few times on the tribune of the lay auditors and *periti* and watched the faces of Tavard, Küng, de Lubac, Gregory Baum, Congar, faces of men between forty and seventy, yet young faces, liberated and open. The expressions of the conservative *periti,* of the feared Balič, and of Guignebert, were set and severe. In the first rows the pious laymen and women auditors, with Jean Guitton and Marie Louise Monnet as commanders-in-chief, seemed to be chosen as reliable secular casts of clerical models. Only the quicksilvery Rosemary Goldie seemed to have an independent muscular response; the reflexes of the others were predictable and conventional.

Each day the discussions in the Council were rising to new heights of liberty and enthusiasm. Bishop Grutka of Gary, Indiana, called for a condemnation of all forms of racial segregation and discrimination. The position of women was pleaded with fire and farsightedness. The education of priests in the seminaries was criticized, and greater openness was defended by Cardinal Suenens. The text of Schema XIII, "The Church and the Modern World," was severely criticized for its much too ecclesiastical language. "It still sounds like a sermon," Cardinal Liénart declared.

On Friday, November 13, 1964, the Pope would once more attend the daily congregation. Patriarch Maximos was concelebrating the

Melchite rite with Patriarch Maximos

Mass according to the Byzantine rite with all the Melchite prelates. Although it took up the whole morning, it was a glorious ceremony of great fervor and beauty. The regal patriarch was surrounded by bishops in stiff golden robes, bestowing blessings with three crossed candles symbolizing the Trinity. The heavenly choirs of the Byzantine rite filled the Latin Basilica. Maximos IV swung his censer over the congregation, the little golden bells tinkling an accompaniment. Supporting himself on his ebony-and-ivory staff, his frail body enveloped in the great golden cloak, elongated by his high, golden bejeweled crown, he seemed like a Byzantine emperor in all his splendor. Yet he had proven often to have a spirit as contemporary and as young as any Council Father, only more articulate and freer and filled with understanding of, and compassion for, his time.

After the Mass was finished, the Pope, who had sat on his throne in full regalia, stony as an idol, arose. Suddenly Monsignor Felici

Father Balič, conservative theologian

spoke into the loudspeaker system. He announced that Pope Paul would donate his tiara, gift of the City of Milan at his coronation, to the poor. Paul VI strode down from his throne carrying the jewel-studded tiara and placed it on the altar. Then he embraced Maximos.

There was a deep stir. Paul VI had again made one of his symbolical, nearly operatic, gestures. "What exactly did it mean?" it was immediately asked. Did it mean a final abdication from all pretenses to papal temporal power? Was the tiara to be melted and the proceeds given as alms? To whom? To the poor in the Oriental diocese of Patriarch Maximos; or as a consolation prize for the disappointing schema on the Oriental Churches? Was this, after all, "blessed" object to be auctioned to obtain the highest possible price for it?

All we know is that it turned up in the hands of Cardinal Spellman as a tribute to American charity toward the poor in all the world. It will be on exhibition in the Vatican Pavilion at the New York World's Fair. . . .

"The Council is really over now," the bishops said in Rome. True, there were still the final votes to follow on the schema of the Church, on collegiality, on the Ecumenical schema, on the Declarations on Religious Liberty and on the non-Christian religions, but it was a foregone conclusion that these votes were assured.

The Arab agitation against the adoption of the Declaration that, none too soon, after two thousand years, would absolve the Jewish people of deicide, was not going to dissuade the vast majority of bishops, even if the Egyptians had threatened schism. "This is not a Council of the Arab League, but of the Church," a bishop said. It had certainly been repeated ad nauseam to all men of goodwill that no political statement was intended in favor of the State of Israel. The Council was not going to act out a new version of *The Deputy* under Arab pressure. No, the Council was over. It had been a huge affirmation of *aggiornamento*. The spirit had triumphed, and the anxious moments, the tensions during maneuvers to hamstring it could be forgotten. The fourth session would finish the work, settle the schema on the Church and the modern world, make it a stronger, clearer, more open schema than even the one presented here.

My Rome exhibition was over, too. It was to open in a museum in Holland within a few days. In order to avoid delays at the customs offices of Italy, France, and Switzerland, I decided to pack all my work into my car and transport it myself.

It was painful to leave this joyous Rome and my friends at the

Lay-Auditrices at The Third Session

Casa Unitas, so delighted with the course the Council had taken. These Dutch, American, Australian, Spanish priests and laymen who formed the avant-garde of the Church had become my intimate friends. I had discovered that my compulsion to draw the Council had not, after all, been a mere "settling of an account" after the interrupted love story of my childhood. Childhood and love story might be far behind me, my dialogue with the Church had continued unabatedly over the years. I had drawn the Council as part of that dialogue and the contact with my new friends had made me aware that, through meditation on the world's religious literature, through distillation of my own life experience, I had all by myself arrived extremely close to where this avant-garde had collectively arrived as members of the Church.

I attended Mass as it was celebrated in utter starkness in the chapel of the Casa Unitas, and experienced the Mass as a fact, not as a symbol; as the encompassing expression of our human solidarity in the face of life, and at the same time of our personal and collective, specifically human relatedness with the Mystery of Being.

I was no longer sure whether I was an outsider inside or an insider outside. . . .

I drove to Holland under the wintry Italian sky, through the hill towns of Umbria seen through sheets of rain, through snowy Alps and dripping Swiss valleys, through the endless undulations of French fields wet under soft low clouds—a still and tender, wintry Europe.

While I was driving, hundreds of the faces I had drawn, of the men I had met, appeared before my inner eye. Snatches of conversation returned and assumed new meanings. Among those bishops of all nationalities, Protestant observers, and theologians: what magnificent human beings I had met! Human beings not corrupted by position or power or prominence, still seeking clarification and ever deeper understanding of themselves, their faith, and their fellowmen. I had found friends among them and had shared their anxieties and their hopes.

I had heard in astonishment and awe the utterances of the bishops who in their overwhelming majority had shown such deep concern for mankind, leaving behind them parochial attitudes and narcissistic self-congratulation. I had seen the enormous mutations that had taken place in these two short years of their self-discovery and the discovery of problems that they had in common but had always faced alone. While listening and while drawing, I had jettisoned my own suspicions and prejudices.

Although not a theologian but simply a man (perhaps theology is not primarily for theologians, as medical science is not meant for medical conferences), I felt I had understood the gains:

The nature of the Church had been reaffirmed as a living spiritual organism instead of as a juridical body. The laity in general, and women in particular, had been recognized in their full human dignity as members of the Church.

The Church had realized its need to rehabilitate not the Jews but itself in its attitude toward the Jews and the non-Catholic religions, and had adopted a declaration which was one of the noblest documents of modern times. It had become aware of the necessity of

The late Cardinal Meyer at the table of the Presidium

continued and open dialogue with the other Christian churches, and also with the non-Christian religions.

It had restored to its bishops a role of responsibility which had been forgotten, and from subalterns had once more made them guardians of its treasure house. It had reinterpreted the revelation on which it rests in terms vital to modern man: the Way, the Truth, and the Life had once again become its central mystery instead of a set of intellectual propositions.

It had started to re-think the vocation, the education, and the life of its priests and religious in terms of our time and of its own source. It was attempting to clarify the biblical foundation of its missionary activity.

There were tokens of a beginning reorganization of the Curia. Had not two noncurial cardinals, Meyer and Lefèbvre, been added to the Holy Office?

There had been many proofs during this Council that the Church is not a monolith. By the end of the third session, the indications were that it could no longer be compared to a tyrannosaurus whose huge armored body, governed by too puny and unadaptable a brain, would be doomed to early extinction in the greatly changed climate of the contemporary world.

The progressive forces of the Church had emphasized man's vocation to become fully human and to lose his terror of loneliness and separateness in a new realization of his shared humanity.

When Cardinal Alfrink emphasized the "human nature of human sexuality" he expressed in concrete terms that man is never abstractly biological, but that in all his functions, and even in his regressions and perversions, he remains human.

Pope John's committed, practical mysticism, his intuitiveness, his universality, his patience without smugness, his prudence without duplicity, had been shared and implemented by the Council as a body. The sacred nature of life had been affirmed anew. Each participant, each observer had been forced to a renewed encounter with himself and his fellowmen. A dying language, contaminated by centuries of compromise, fanaticism, abuse, equivocation, and hypocrisy, had been purified and revivified and could once more communicate.

The progressive majority had moved toward a new confidence in human potentiality. No longer inclined to condemn all intellectual

Oriental observers received by Cardinal Bea

curiosity as spiritual pride, it was ready to marshal all truly human forces at large in the world toward a full and timely re-affirmation of the essential message of Christianity. Perhaps it could even be seen as a new phase of that spiritual revolution which between 1500 B.C. and the beginning of the Christian Era had shaped our world through the inspiration of the great religious geniuses: Ikhnaton, Moses and the Hebrew Prophets, the Greek thinkers, the Buddha and Lao-Tse, Zarathustra and the authors of the Vedanta, and finally the Christ—and thus to stem our trend toward the final debasement and estrangement of men in our culture. There had been an outpouring of the Spirit. There had been a new Pentecost. The spirit had triumphed.

The hard core of "conservatives" were perhaps not true conservatives at all, but regressives in a panic, desperately holding on to

[233]

archaic forms of a past historical period, protecting their identity by clinging to their self-image of omnipotence and omniscience. They were destructive, as are all regressives, of what they tried so desperately to defend.

They were, fortunately, outnumbered.

I had just reached Holland when nightmare news came over the radio of my car. Something inconceivable had happened. In the last three days of the third session, the assured vote of the Declaration on Religious Liberty had been made impossible in the most incriminating circumstances. It had clearly been the work of a Roman *combinazione*. The document had been "railroaded," as it had been a year ago by a clever move. A small group of bishops (between one and two hundred) under the always ready Bishop Carli of Segni had claimed that it could not be voted on because it had come "too late to be studied." The Presidium promised a preliminary vote to determine whether the Declaration should nevertheless be voted on Thursday, November 19, 1964. But on that Thursday Cardinal Tisserant announced peremptorily that there would be no vote at all, and that the Declaration would have to wait once more until the fourth session. It was a weird repetition of the nightmarish end of the Second Session.

Religious liberty could wait! A petition of the great majority of the Council, on the initiative of Bishop Reh, and Cardinals Meyer, Ritter, and Léger, was laid aside by the Pope, whose own theologian had stressed the vital importance of the declaration for a continued dialogue. It became a crisis of authority. A few days before he was to promulgate collegiality, this seemed an anticollegial and anticonciliar act.

Bishop De Smedt of Bruges, who read his introduction to the sabotaged declaration with tears in his voice, received an ovation as if he were a tenor after his first aria.

The Declaration on the Jews was allowed to be voted on by an overwhelming majority. Yet it could not be promulgated, because of the number of reservations and was still vulnerable. It was said that after the uproar about religious liberty nobody dared to postpone it again as well.

To make matters worse, the crucially important schema on the Church had been provided with a *nota explicitiva,* which only at the last moment had "on higher authority" been revealed to constitute part of the schema itself. The bishops had no choice but to accept this blow, for the *nota explicitiva* could be used to greatly reduce the implications of the already narrowly limited collegiality. It emphasizes once more—as if Vatican I were not enough—the pope as the supreme arbiter: without his consent the "exercise of collegiality" remains a dead letter. It was explained from various sides that the *nota* was couched in such subtle language that it would have little value beyond providing theologians with material for even subtler squabbles, and that its only object was to allay the anxieties of the minority. It was indeed so subtle that it did not appear in the edition of the schema proclaimed during the final session.

"All we can still believe of collegiality," it was lamented, "is the collegiality between the Pope and the Curia." This may be an unfair and bitter exaggeration. But many saw Pope Paul's action as an indication that his heart was not in "collegiality." Two years of deliberation by the bishops resulting in an almost unanimous vote could apparently still be negated without consultation and even without openly involving the authority of the pope. At any rate, the comfortable theory, so often repeated in Rome, that the Pope never acts except in accord with his bishops had been exploded.

Even more serious, perhaps, because of its effect on the outside world, was the fact that the schema *De Oecumenismo* had been "corrected" by order of the same "higher authority," and so it became a package deal that the bishops had to vote on under duress: either no schema or a somewhat mutilated schema in which the Protestants were, among other things, suddenly deemed only to "seek" Christ in the Scriptures instead of "finding" him there. Although it had not been changed in substance, petty corrections gave the schema an after-taste that was anti-observer, anti-Council and anti-Pope John. Especially in this form of a last-minute maneuver, it was a slap in the face of the Protestants, which made even such a friend of the Church as Professor Cullmann call it "a move of the worst possible taste."

As if all this were not enough, the Pope announced that he was going to promulgate Mary as "Mother of the Church"; ironically, on the same day he would promulgate the collegiality of pope and bishops, bishops who had solemnly rejected any further pious-poetic

excitement in the Aula ...

titles for the Virgin Mary. This move neutralized to a certain extent the impact of the ecumenical decree, and may well serve to widen the gap between Protestants and Catholics instead of narrowing it. It had been the clearly expressed wish of the majority of the bishops to place Marian teaching, to the greatest possible extent, in a truly biblical context. No one demands the abolition of popular, ethnic Catholicism but its coexistence with or tolerance for its enlightened mutations.

"If the Church were vital enough now, there would be a schism," it was being repeated in Rome. I heard it when in my despair I called my friends long-distance. There was a great deal of noise in the background. I heard singing and bursts of laughter.

"What on earth are you celebrating?" I gasped.

"Oh," the priest said, "this is a wake, my friend. The Council is dead and so we are all having a drink. What else is there to do?" He told me that at the last meeting of the observers a deeply sad Monsignor Willebrands had asked his audience to "remain with us in this dark hour."

On November 20, 1964, a great deal of the immense work of the Council seemed to have become nullified, if not condemned. Great hopes went up in smoke.

I had left Rome in a mood of exultation. During this third session I had felt I was witnessing an apotheosis.

What had started as a rescue operation had resulted in new, applicable formulations of the ancient values of Christianity in a true rebirth, a great movement of spiritual renascence in which I felt I had participated.

Now I shared a bottomless, bitter sorrow with my friends in Rome who "belonged." It was they who would have to watch the *sedia* again, the Noble Guards, the discreetly victorious smiles of the Curia monsignors, the crestfallen bishops who had no doubt dutifully applauded when the Pope once more stressed the primacy and devoted the full latter half of his speech to the "Mother of the Church" as a send-off for his bishops returning into diaspora. He had not announced the establishment of a "senate of bishops"; he had not set a date for the fourth session.

Pope Paul had—at any rate, for the time being—made himself the overlord of the Council and had isolated himself from it. He had not only failed to express its consensus but had acted against it. He had infringed on that "holy liberty" which was its very raison d'être. He had chosen—although discreetly instead of openly, as was his right—the side of a handful of diehards instead of making his wishes publicly known when they could still be discussed and perhaps voted on. He had shocked and estranged the great majority of the Council and all those who during Pope John's reign had discovered or rediscovered their deep kinship with the Church and their trust in it. He had allowed questionable maneuvers under the klieg lights of modern publicity in his "open Council" and had allowed *coups de théatre* so unbecoming to a spiritual community that all the stereotypes of anti-Catholic propaganda could suddenly be mobilized again.

The shock wave of indignation and profound sorrow that had swept through St. Peter's and into the world (insofar as it was still interested in the Council and took it seriously) has not subsided. The Council is not dead, but it is suffering and passing through its dark night.

As the months passed and the emotional strain of those last black days receded, it was possible to recalculate the profits and losses once more.

Bishop Willebrands

The greatest gain was the continuing struggle of the Church for its own soul. The dialogue, hardly begun, had already wrought deep changes, a deepening awareness of what the Church essentially is, and of the requirements of its true universality and catholicity. This dialogue, as well as the process of clarification of the transition from a curial to a collegial form of leadership, was continuing. The concept of the Church as the people of God had re-established the dignity of the laity. However ludicrous the tiara's destination, this symbol of earthly might had been surrendered, to all appearances.

That such changes could not take place without conflict and pain became even clearer. The curial privileges dated back to pre-Christian Rome: it was too naïve to expect them to be tamely surrendered. The Pope's solicitude for those closest to him in background seemed more forgivably human. Was his stance perhaps one of compelling the majority to exert pressure? His function, after all, is different from that of Pope John, who had to get the inert Church in motion. If Pope Paul waits to be moved by the great momentum, by the will to reform, which now has swept through the Church, waits to be persuaded by signs of its unanimity and will, he might be acting understandably, even wisely.

In retrospect even his refusal to have a vote on religious liberty may have then been to the good: only the last session will show it. Only if it should negate the Declarations on religious liberty and the Jews have we a right to despair, for then it will be clear that the Church dissociates itself from the spiritual life of our time.

But an irreparable loss was that the luminous atmosphere of trust and optimism created by Pope John had now been contaminated with suspicions and doubts. A different atmosphere had developed, notwithstanding all suave efforts to hide it.

"We have to accept this atmosphere and understand it," a cynical young Northern European bishop explained. "The curial dictum that 'popes die and councils go, but we Italians will go on forever' may yet be disproved. But for the moment they obviously still know how to outmaneuver us. To them, we are naïve, starry-eyed, semi-Protestant utopians. We are dealing with an Italian mentality, trained for centuries in manipulation, barter, compromise, and sharp dealing, camouflaged by good manners and charm. What we understand by spirituality is here nearly always secondary.

"Collegiality has been accepted? Fine! Now let us give its opponents—people like Monsignor de Proença Sigaud of Brazil, who holds that collegiality has no foundation in the Bible and sees it as a charter of indiscipline in the Church—some satisfaction. After all, these are our allies! We'll give them a *nota explicativa.*

"They are all set on ecumenism? Can't be helped. But let us add some 'corrections' to please our staunchest supporters in Italy and Spain. It will hurt the Protestants? Oh, well, they'll come around. Charity begins at home.

"The Spaniards and Italians who oppose 'religious liberty' (as well they may!) will be pleased by a little victory: they have deserved it! It will make the Americans angry? Why not give them the tiara to play with?

"The Arabs are indignant about the Declaration on the Jews? Let's make a stopover in Beirut and appease them. After all, it is not yet proclaimed!

"The maximalists (especially the Portuguese, whom we have already angered by the pilgrimage to India) were deeply hurt by the tone of the Marian deliberations and the defeat of all their efforts to make the Virgin Mary into a Co-Redemptrix: we'll give them and the Poles a great concelebration and proclaim Mary as Mother of the Church!

"Thus unity is preserved and all will be pleased in the end. . . .

"Pope Paul," explained the skeptical bishop, "intends nothing but the best. He is spending himself in doing it and looks like a ghost. He has a superhuman task and he is fulfilling it beyond his strength according to his conscience: a very Catholic, but, don't forget, also a very Italian, and what is more, a very Roman conscience. He might surprise us again."

The Council had accomplished—within and for the Church itself —more than even the boldest had dared to hope at its beginning. It had chosen paths of liberty, justice, peace and mercy. This was one aspect of the grandiose spectacle of which I had made hundreds of drawings and felt completely identified with.

There had been another aspect, however, that had shocked me deeply and that I tried to catch in my drawings too.

The forces of regression in the Church—not to be confused with true conservatism—although numerically weak, had been tactically strong enough to subvert Pope John's vision by subtle obstruction if not sabotage. They had presented a shocking spectacle of intrigue and conspiracy, jockeying for power, dilly-dallying on essential moral issues, evasions of truth.

"Contemporary man," Hans Küng said, "can forgive nearly all sins except unveracity and hypocrisy."

What would be the effect on the minds of aware members of the Church and those close to it? How far did it offset the magnificent accomplishments of the Council?

One thing was certain: up till now the Council had failed to give human society that new charter for its regeneration Pope John had seen in his vision.

We had seen the Holy Spirit hovering over the *aula*. When it was absent, the dryness and the desolation had been frightening.

No one can now transform the Dove into a parrot and force it back into a gilded cage.

After Pope John XXIII the ultimate victory of the regressives would announce to countless people that the Church has no sustenance to offer and that it was abdicating as a moral and spiritual force. It was facing its most crucial test.

Modern men have considerable difficulty in accepting a church as a home for their spiritual yearnings. Their relationship to the eternal is apt to find different, less rigid, less organized modes of expression. Insofar as they can adjust to the idea of a church, the Catholic Church, with its hierarchy, its sacraments, its liturgy, is a difficult choice at best. Yet when Pope John showed in his person, his words, his deeds, that aspect of the Catholic Church founded on love and tolerance, brotherliness and universality, dignity and reason, all constructive forces in a tormented world rallied around him. The Church cannot now afford to repeat the mistakes of the sixteenth century and allow the forces of fanaticism and regression to take over, for the world will turn away more radically than ever before.

How our time yearns for a prophet, Pope John's life and death have proven. Under him, in mid-twentieth century, the Church suddenly made sense again.

The sages and the thinkers of the Church—those whose pains and labors have prepared this Council, liberated the Church from age-

Church Fathers looming over Pope Paul

old chains, from delusions, from inertia—will not stop thinking. At the same time, in universities and seminaries—Catholic and Protestant, Jewish and Buddhist—new generations of thinkers are being formed who will continue their search for the common ground, common to all those who discern the transcendent values in the transiency of our lives.

If we are resigned to collective suicide, all those efforts are of course futile. But if there is a future for us men, our trend toward regression, delusion and death *must* be reversed; we shall have to opt for man's potential for redemption, for the fullness of life on earth.

If there is to be a future, the Spirit will have to be proclaimed in ever greater liberty and in clearer words that at last close the gap between the dead language of conventional theology and the living languages of men. Only then can we translate the criteria of our reality and our delusions contained in the great visions of the Enlightened of all times into the living languages of new times and new cultures. It might well be a newly formulated Christology, a new anthropology of the divine in man to which all can assent, and that will point at the nature of our full-grown humanity and our liberation from triviality and cruelty, frivolity and stupidity, infantilism and self-destruction.

This was the longing and the effort I had felt behind all these utterances of Vatican II, an effort to overcome all conventional and traditional limitations and to transmit a universally valid message that would deepen our meditation on ourselves and our oneness in the Great Mystery of Being.

As to the love story that started this book . . . the ending is not as simple as in a cheap novel. The confession of my personal love story is only interesting insofar as it mirrors modern man's relationship to spiritual authority. We have grown older and know that love is not enough. There has to be compatibility, there has to be a respect that is mutual and unconditional. There has to be freedom of communication, adult and continuous, the possibility of mutual questioning on the most profound and sensitive points in complete openness and without a childish fear of parental reprimand or indignant rejection.

Above all there must be trust and the justification of trust. It must be clear beyond a doubt that spiritual tyranny, social callousness, demands for a servile respect for authority, distortion of truth for purposes of pedagogy and manipulation are things of the past. They have to be replaced by a true relatedness in terms of the evangelical veracity and charity John XXIII stood for.

At stake in the onrush of the moral, political, technological revolution we are living through is not the mere survival of a structure, but the revivification of the religious attitude toward life. This attitude is not merely relevant, but centrally indispensable to life in our time. We either live in realization of the ultimate meaning of our lives, or repress at our peril the experience of the Numinous, the sacred ground of our being. Then we embrace the alternatives: the idolatry of technology, the new polytheism of success, acquisition, the new harvest. The great prophet Pope John continues to speak: brutalized society, ready at any time to automate itself off the cosmic map.

At what point does the Church of the twentieth century reject man in his spiritual quest? When does she consider him in his search for transcendental truth, for the totality of his human condition, as her member, her enemy, her ally?

The Council continues. Regardless of the hoped-for *aggiornamento* or the despair that it may bring, the Council will begin in earnest only after the last words of the final ceremony have echoed through St. Peter's. Then the Council too must die, to bring forth the new harvest. The great prophet Pope John continues to speak: "When truth reigns, charity is law. The Council now beginning rises in the Church like daybreak. It is now only dawn."

INDEX

Index

ABOUT THE AUTHOR

FREDERICK FRANCK is an artist and writer whose drawings and paintings have been exhibited widely in both his native Holland and America. His work may be found in the permanent collections of a score of museums here and abroad. He became an American citizen in 1945.

Franck obtained medical and dental doctorates both in Europe and America. Recently the University of Pittsburgh conferred upon him the degree of Doctor of Fine Arts, Honoris Causa.

He worked with Dr. Albert Schweitzer during three consecutive summers. Three of the eight books he has written, including *Days with Albert Schweitzer,* resulted from his African travels.

His drawings of the Vatican Council were done in 1962, 1963 and 1964. The late Pope John XXIII conferred upon Franck the Medal of His Pontificate.

Dr. Franck and his wife make their home in New York City in a studio once inhabited by Edgar Allan Poe. They also own a farmhouse near Warwick, New York, where the artist is converting the ruins of a watermill into an interdenominational chapel of peace, *"Pacem in Terris,"* dedicated to Pope John.